MAD ABOUT THE BOYS

CLAIRE BLAKE

MAD ABOUT THE BOYS

MY LIFE AS TAKE THAT'S BIGGEST FAN

JOHN BLAKE

Published by John Blake Publishing Ltd,
3 Bramber Court, 2 Bramber Road,
London W14 9PB, England

www.blake.co.uk

First published in hardback in 2008

ISBN: 978-1-84454-583-4

British Library Cataloguing-in-Publication Data:

A catalogue record for this book is available from the British Library.

Design by www.envydesign.co.uk

Printed in the UK by CPI William Clowes Beccles NR34 7TL

1 3 5 7 9 10 8 6 4 2

Papers used by John Blake Publishing are natural, recyclable products made from
wood grown in sustainable forests. The manufacturing processes conform to the
environmental regulations of the country of origin.

Every attempt has been made to contact the relevant copyright-holders,
but some were unobtainable. We would be grateful if the appropriate people
could contact us.

Firstly, I would like to thank Take That for all the great times you gave and especially the effort you have always put into your music and performance to make it so special and enjoyable for us. I would like to say an extra-special thank you to Gary, I have really appreciated your kindness and all the fun times I had on your two tours!

Thank you to all of the girls who have enjoyed Take That with me and shared in the quest to find them – JoJo, Lisa, Lorraine, Kim, Eileen, Tracy, Lucy, Debbie, Tina, Gemma, Judith, Kat, Nicky, Hayley and my mum!

Thank you to my dad for inspiring me to write a book and telling me that I was good enough.

A big thank you to Jan at the Take That Appreciation website for running a true and fair website for so many years and keeping us all up to date with the latest Take That news (even when it was scarce!).

Finally, a big thank you to Ben xx

CONTENTS

1

POPS TOUR AND COPTHORNE, DUDLEY

It all started innocently enough. After being rather taken by the song 'Babe', I'd begun to read a few interviews with Take That and enjoyed a couple of their posters. Soon, I had a video marked 'TT' by the recorder and would look out for their appearances on shows such as the BBC's *Live & Kicking* and *The O-Zone*. At that point I would never have considered actually meeting them. With Take That, there was sort of the impression that it was impossible to get anywhere near them, that they were untouchable. Sure, there were thousands of screaming girls attempting it through metal barriers and perhaps one or two of them may have even got to touch Mark Owen's arm or something, but you could never actually get to speak to them meaningfully – could you?

The first time I was in the same room as Take That was in September 1994. They had reached the Birmingham NEC for a run of sell-out concerts on their 'Corn Pops' tour (sponsored

by Kellogg's Corn Pops). When I say 'room', I use the term loosely, as it was, in fact, an arena seating around 12,000 screaming fellow fans but nonetheless when you have never met them before this seems like a really big deal! My first-ever Take That concert ticket wasn't great: I was seated about halfway from the stage. The only saving grace was the fact that when the boys did the Beatles medley on the platform suspended from the ceiling about halfway back I would get a decent view. I cannot imagine nor have I ever experienced a crowd more excited than a Take That audience before, during and after a concert.

The atmosphere is electric; every time a roadie or technician moves on the stage a huge scream can be heard and every so often Mexican waves go around the arena and people start to stamp their feet very loudly on the ground. By the time the lights finally go down for show time the noise is almost deafening. This is it; those five guys you dream about are actually about to walk on to the stage and you're going to see them in the flesh! It was this very feeling that I was to become hooked on like a drug and, just like a junkie, no matter how much it would cost, I would go back for more and more.

The band rose up from underneath the stage and absorbed the incredible noise from their army of adoring fans before beginning the first song, 'Satisfied', another show for them and a life-changing moment for me. I watched in awe as the five members of Take That put on their unbelievable show. This was no ordinary boy band, far from it; these guys had something special, a chemistry, a magic that had not been seen since the Beatles and has not been seen since. They didn't just get up on stage and sing their hits (which they could have done, people would still have paid to see them); they really put on a show and they gave their all. Take That as a five-piece were really something to behold.

On the way home in the car, my best friend JoJo (who also loved the boys) and I relived the concert and shared with each other all of the best bits ('Give Good Feeling', need I say more?). She asked if I'd seen the bit where Mark picked up one of the many cuddly toys that had been thrown on to the stage and if I had noticed Robbie winking at someone in the front row. By the time we got home we were still buzzing and we wanted more, but, with all the remaining concerts on the tour sold out, we had to resign ourselves to the fact that for now it was all over.

A few days later I was returning home from college and I decided to stop off at JoJo's house. Her mum told me that she had gone to the Take That concert with another friend as she had managed to get last-minute tickets! In the middle of my major fit of jealousy I called the box office (thinking it a waste of time) to ask if they had any tickets left for that night's show

Oh how Take That loved their Corn Pops!

and quite calmly the lady told me that I could have a seat right next to the stage in an area called 'restricted view'. With my heart racing, I bought the ticket and, with only an hour until the concert began, I had to run to get a bus to Birmingham. I was so anxious and excited to get there that I was willing the bus to go faster despite the fact that it seemed to get stuck at every single traffic light on the way just to wind me up.

Once I'd finally got to the concert and picked up my ticket, I made my way to the seat and was shocked at how close I was to the stage. It was a side-on view, which is what the lady had meant by 'restricted view', but nonetheless I would still take this position over the halfway-back view I had had just a few nights before. Lulu had just come on stage to sing a few numbers, and as she came over to my side she smiled and I got excited, thinking that if she could see me then so could Take That.

The concert was absolutely amazing. One by one each member of the band came over on to the side platforms and it felt as though if I just reached out far enough then I could touch them. In fact, the following day I called and called until finally I managed to get the 'restricted view' tickets again; this time I took my younger sister along with me and she caught Gary Barlow's discarded bottle of Evian as thrown from the stage! There was also a girl a few seats away from me who threw a necklace or chain of some sort to Robbie, who caught it, looked at it and then threw it back to her!

The day after that, JoJo and I had the idea that we could go to the NEC in the afternoon to try to see the band arriving.

When we showed up it became clear that we weren't the only ones who had had this particular brainwave! There was quite a crowd standing opposite a side entrance to the NEC and it wasn't long before we started chatting to some of the girls there. They all had stories to tell of how they had met Take That and how they had been to their houses and camped outside. They remarked how nice and tolerant the lads' families were for putting up with it but how some fans had left graffiti on the gates and pavements and some had even climbed into their gardens!

One girl that we got talking to had met Gary that morning and was showing off a photo of him. I asked where she had met him and she told us that the band were staying at the Copthorne hotel in Dudley. She told us that she and a few friends had got a taxi to follow Take That's Espace all the way to the hotel the other night, costing them £40, and that she had been to almost every show so far on that particular tour. She said the guys were really nice and friendly and that she had got their autographs. I really wanted to go to this hotel; I mean, this was amazing, I didn't think it was possible to meet them like that! I had to go and see for myself. After the fourth concert that I had been to at the NEC, it was time to step it up a notch, so off went JoJo and I with our new pal, Lisa, to the hotel in Dudley.

It took ages to get there. Take That had been quite clever to stay a good 45 minutes' drive from the concert venue, making it harder for fans to track them down. On arrival it seemed fairly quiet. There were about 50 or 60 fans at the front of the hotel and two security guys (who we later knew as James and Paul) came out to tell us that the boys were tired and would not be coming out to meet fans that evening.

A few people left, then a few more and a few more, and, when there were only about 20 of us remaining, out walked Mark Owen from the front of the hotel! His hair was short and spiky and he looked very tanned and incredibly handsome in the flesh. I asked him if he would sign my jeans, but he replied, 'I'm sorry, I can't,' before James informed me that he was not signing any autographs that night. He shook my hand anyway and smiled. Mark seemed very concerned that we were outside in the dark and cold, and urged us all to go home and get warm! Once he had gone back into the hotel, some of the girls were crying and hugging each other and everyone was pretty hyper that Mark had just been out to talk to them.

With not much time to calm down, Jason Orange was next out of the hotel. He went along, shaking everyone's hands, and when he got to me he asked me how I was and I said that I was fine (which admittedly was playing down my elevated, on cloud nine position ever so slightly). Jason went back inside and I couldn't believe that I had just met two members of Take That; it was really exciting to have found them when my perception had been that you could never get near to them. But if I had thought that was good, there was just so much more to come!

I called the hotel and tried to book a room. I figured that we needed to get inside the place and, with security checking whether or not people were residents by looking at their key cards, there was no way that you could get in unless you were staying there. That night they were fully booked but they had a room available for the next three nights, which of course I snapped up. I did feel anxious that I didn't have the funds to pay for this four-star hotel but the desire to be inside was just too much and so I accepted the fact that I would be going hideously over my credit limit to stay there. To keep warm we walked around the hotel a few times by the canal, where there were some bars and restaurants. There were quite a few girls huddled up with sleeping bags who had decided to camp out and, as we passed, we would smile or say hello; we were all there for the same reason, united by a desire to be closer to our favourite band.

By the early hours most of the people who had decided not to camp out had gone home and we went down to the front of the hotel to sit on the steps. Through the glass doors we could see Mark near the entrance to the bar, chatting to a blonde girl, and Robbie getting into a lift with a brunette, only to return fifteen minutes later with her and go back to the bar. At some point two girls who had just been talking to Robbie came outside and told us that he was too drunk to come and speak to us and that he was sorry! After a while, and with security no longer manning the doors, I felt brave enough to go inside and ask the man at reception if I could use the toilet. He said I could, and, on the way round, I had to squeeze past Robbie and Mark (shame for me!), who were chatting to yet another girl. I glanced down and saw that Robbie had his hand up this girl's rather short skirt – nice!

I realised that not only was it possible to meet Take That but also that some of these girls were actually sleeping with them too. You have to remember that at the time Take That had a very squeaky-clean image, so this did come as quite a shock! Somehow we made it through the rest of the night and once it was 7 a.m. we managed to find our way home on a few buses and pack furiously for the next three exciting nights of which we had just had a tantalising preview.

Eventually, we were back at the hotel. We were so nervous because at any moment we could bump into one of the band –

Huge crowd outside the Copthorne, as seen from our hotel room window.

the adrenalin was really pumping. Our room was absolutely gorgeous and had the added bonus of being front-facing, meaning we could keep an eye out for the comings and goings at the front of the hotel. In fact, within minutes of our arrival, we heard a scream from outside and flashes began to go off. From our privileged position we could see that Mark had gone outside and was chatting to the fans again. I would have guessed that there were over a hundred girls outside the hotel. A rumour had gone round that this was largely due to the fact that a local radio station had revealed Take That's location!

As there was no concert that night, we looked forward to an exciting evening in the hotel bar with Take That and we began trying on lots of different outfits, applying make-up and doing our hair. Another huge scream could be heard from outside the hotel, but this time it was not anyone going out to have a chat with the fans: it was all of them, in the Espace – the boys had gone out! An awful feeling swept over us; the wonderful night in the bar was no more. Nonetheless, we went down to the reception area of the hotel and waited. If you are a fan then generally the foyer is where you will spend most of your time as this area usually gives you a vantage point over the hotel entrance, lifts and bar area.

A good couple of hours went by and fans amused themselves by talking about Take That and speculating on when they might return. Another scream was heard from outside, again accompanied by flashes, although it was now dark so we couldn't make out much through the glass. As nothing occurred on the inside, we surmised that they had used a side entrance to return to their rooms. The tension and excitement in the lobby was palpable and it wasn't long before the lift doors opened and out came Jason in an Adidas tracksuit, accompanied by a security guy, and they walked into the bar. Coincidentally, it was just at this moment that I decided I needed another drink and so I walked up to the bar (which was heaving with scantily clad girls) and waited to be served.

There was a mirror behind the bar and in the reflection I could see Jason pulling up a high stool quite close behind me, then sitting down on it and pulling the hood of his tracksuit top up over his head. I couldn't resist turning round to look and, when I did, he smiled at me; I smiled back and then turned back round to face the bar. Next in was Mark, who took up a position close to me at the bar; again, I could see him waiting to be served in the mirror. Robbie was next in, and I remember thinking to myself, 'Hey, I'm stood in a bar with three of Take That!' I finally got my drinks and went back to the foyer, having to walk behind Jason as I left; he was going very slowly as girls kept stopping him to talk. There was a girl in front of me who was wearing a skirt so short that you could actually see her butt cheeks, but, rather than being impressed by it, Mark and Robbie were pulling faces behind her back! None of them stayed in the bar too long – I think it was just far too busy in there.

By 11 p.m., under licensing laws the hotel manager was at liberty to throw all the non-residents out of the bar, making the hotel much quieter. I continued to sit in the foyer with JoJo, getting more and more drunk, until, at 1 a.m. just as we were discussing going to bed, the lift doors opened and out walked Gary and Robbie, chatting to each other as they entered the now much quieter bar. After a while, we followed and once more stood, waiting to be served. We noticed that playing cards had been stuck to the ceiling and, as my rather buxom friend in her low-cut top leaned back to have a look, Robbie couldn't help but stare at her chest. He came over to stand next to us and started doing some cheesy dance moves to the music, so I threw my handbag on to the floor and said, 'There you go, dance round this!'

Gary with James and Paul outside the Copthorne.

He laughed and for a few moments we were all dancing around my handbag. I wasn't nervous any more, though – the many vodka and oranges I had consumed relieved me of that.

A drunken Gary stood up from his seat and, with slurred speech, wished us all a goodnight several times before eventually leaving the bar. JoJo and I went to sit down and Robbie followed, asking us if we had any Silk Cut cigarettes. We told him we only had Marlboro Lights and he pulled a face and went to ask at another table. Lisa had told us that the band had been instructed by security not to accept any cigarettes from fans unless in an unopened carton for security reasons. Soon Robbie returned to our table, but this time he wasn't after cigarettes but my drink! He picked up my vodka and orange and asked who it belonged to, and so I told him it was mine. He proceeded to ask if he could have it and I told him he could; he then asked me if I had spat in it. We all laughed, and then off he went, drinking my drink – cheeky sod! It's always puzzled me why Robbie would have needed to take my drink that night, whether he wanted to speak to us because he was lonely or whether he had exhausted his own nightly allowance of alcohol and didn't want his management to know how much he was drinking is anyone's guess. By 3.30 a.m., he had gone back to his room and soon after that we too went to bed.

The following evening, the hotel was even more packed out with fans, but nonetheless Gary was the first down to the bar. I went up to the room to tell JoJo and she said that she would be down in a minute. On my way back, the lift doors opened and Jason was inside with two security guys. I got in, but one of them said that there were too many people in the lift. 'Out you get then, Jase!' I cheekily responded; he smiled and then I turned around and got out.

The next lift I got into had two girls inside and they had pushed the button for Take That's floor. But there was no way that you could actually get on to their floor – security guys would always be sitting at the lift exits to guard against that! Once up there, we saw Mark, who was waiting to get into the lift, and on seeing that it was full of girls he ducked behind a nearby wall until we had gone. Back at the reception there were about fifty or so girls just crowded around these lifts and I became one of them as I waited for JoJo to come down. Robbie came out of the toilets to my left, said hello and asked if I was all right – I guess he had recognised me from the previous night.

Mark came out of the lift eventually and attempted to get through the crowd with the help of two security guards just to get to the bar! By now everyone except Howard was there, but it was absolute pandemonium and heavily overcrowded. One by one, they decided to leave. Jason noticed me again and did a double take as he must have recognised me from the lift, but he was being whisked off by security back up to the calm of the fourth floor, and as Gary retired for the evening a girl managed to give him some roses. He told her that he really loved roses, again slurring his words from one too many Southern Comforts! Not a very successful evening considering what we had seen the previous few nights; we wished that we had found out about the place sooner.

The final day arrived, and as JoJo and I hung around the reception area, another band – Ice-T – checked into the hotel. Two of Ice's entourage came to chat to us and asked if we wanted to go to his show that evening and invited us on to their tour bus. We politely refused as we had important Take That spotting to do! In hindsight, I wish I had gone with them, of course – it would have been much more fun! Anyway, it was only later that I realised that the two guys that we were speaking to were not the entourage, but actual band members, and had we gone with them then we could have joined the party they later held on the exclusive fourth floor that we knew at least Robbie was attending!

A disappointing evening by all accounts: the most we saw of Take That was the *O-Zone*'s 'Sure' special that we watched in our room!

The following day, Take That were all set to check out of the hotel, and fans gathered inside and outside of the hotel in their hundreds; it was really quite incredible. We were told that if we made space for the lads they would come through the lobby and say goodbye but, as Robbie began to make his way through (oddly wearing a shower cap and fake plaits), the fans surged towards him. He told them to stop as they wouldn't be able to get through, but the temptation must have been too much and the pushing continued. With this, Robbie got inside the lift again and they escaped through a back exit. The experience had been so exciting and so beyond expectation that I just knew that I had to do it again – and soon.

2

'NOBODY ELSE' TOUR AND CONRAD, LONDON

Towards the end of 1994, Take That provided only a couple of opportunities for us to meet them in the UK, both of which we seized. One was the Princess of Wales's Concert of Hope at Wembley, where we exchanged our rather poor two-thirds-of-the-way-back seats to 'restricted view' positions by complaining to a security guy so much that he let us through. I can't remember exactly what we said, but at venues with huge tiers heading skywards you can always say that you suffer from vertigo and hadn't realised how high up your seats were positioned – that usually does the trick! Restricted-view seats are normally available and these are usually where the friends and family of the band sit so you never know who you may be lucky enough to end up talking to! At the Concert of Hope we sat with the band's manager Nigel Martin-Smith and the boy band EYC. Also, from this side-on position, we could see the lads getting

changed backstage and I remember seeing Mark in his underpants – phew!

A few days later, the guys picked up several *Smash Hits* awards at the Poll Winners' Party at the Docklands Arena. The show was amazing and afterwards we met up with Lisa again. She told us that the band were staying at the Conrad hotel in Chelsea Harbour but unfortunately this information had come too late; we were out of money and had to return home.

With this insatiable hunger to meet the band again, thoughts turned to their next tour, which was set to take place in August 1995. At the time I was working as a valet waitress in a casino but two days before the tour began I quit my job – because they very unreasonably wouldn't give me the time off I needed to go and see Take That! I packed my bags and set off up to Manchester with JoJo and Lisa in her tiny little Ford Fiesta, slightly unnerved that I was leaving myself jobless and with only one month's salary to live on but drunk on the anticipation of spending some time with the boys again! Even Lisa had purposefully taken a job at the Birmingham NEC box office just to get good seats for the boys' concerts – only to learn that, on what was to be their

Huge crowds await Take That's arrival at the Nynex.

final tour, they were just going to play at the Manchester Nynex and Earls Court!

We had decided to go to Manchester early in the hope that we could meet them during their final rehearsals at the Nynex. We parked up and walked round to the side entrance of the venue; both sides of the road were covered by what must have been a good three to four hundred girls, who had all made this same trip for a glimpse of Take That. Some were waiting in cars to follow them as they left so as to find out the hotel that they were staying in and we decided to do the same. Hours of anticipation later and we heard the usual scream accompanied by a flurry of camera flashes and this was our cue to start the engine. Howard, driving a convertible Mercedes, sped past and, after a hurried three-point turn, we followed. We could barely keep up with him – he was driving at about 70 miles an hour and even speeding straight through red lights, and of course in the madness and pure adrenalin of the moment we pursued, desperate to learn which hotel they were staying in. Once out on to a more main road and probably sensing the danger involved, both for himself and his fans, Howard pulled over and turned to us, asking us to please stop following him. We apologised, but, just as he drove off unaccompanied, another car full of girls came by asking us which way he went, and then off they went to try their luck at catching up with him.

We returned to the venue and parked up, ready to give chase to the next member of the band to leave, which turned out to be Jason, again in a convertible and looking gorgeous in a pair of sunglasses. Jason didn't seem to mind being followed as much; he even smiled at us in his rear-view mirror as we drove through Manchester. He pulled into the drive of a rather nice-looking building in Salford Quays and parked up before going inside. We were really excited to have found the hotel and I looked for the reception so that I could book us a room. A man in a suit approached me and asked if I needed any help. 'Yes, I'm just looking for the reception area, please – I wish to book a room,' I said.

He looked very puzzled, as he responded, 'This is a residential block of apartments.' We had actually made it to Jason Orange's home and not the band's hotel!

Now, in the hope of preventing any future car crashes, there is a much simpler way to find out which hotel your favourite band or star is staying in. The band members themselves will, of course, use pseudonyms to prevent being called at all hours of the day and night by people asking to be connected to their rooms. A couple Gary has used are Ivor Biggen and Dick Grayson (the latter being the real name of Robin from *Batman* and the former I'm sure you can work out!). However, the musicians and other entourage do not use pseudonyms, so all you need to know is the drummer or tour manager's name (which can be found in the tour programme) and then just call the hotel, asking to check a reservation. The safest bet is to go for the manager as the musicians sometimes stay in a different hotel. In each major city there will be a handful of hotels that are most likely to house the band during their stay; there is little use, for example, in contacting the local Travelodge!

During the evening before the first day of the 'Nobody Else' tour, we waited outside Jason's flat and chatted to some other fans. Some of them knew the hotel but had given it a code word of 'Milkybar' so that they could maybe have Take That all to themselves. Another group of fans rode around in a Jeep, acting rather intimidating and showing off that they were going to the band's hotel, but of course they wouldn't tell us which one. Frustrated, we gave up for the evening; we had a long day ahead of us trying to get tickets for yet another officially 'sold-out' show.

The following morning we made our way back to the Manchester Nynex and spent the day between the box office and the side entrance, which was swarming with excited girls, all high in anticipation of the opening night of this brand-new tour and the first without Robbie. Following an impromptu performance with Oasis on stage at Glastonbury (clearly inebriated, with bleached-blonde hair and a blacked-out front tooth) Robbie had decided he no longer wanted to be with the squeaky cleanness that was Take That. He offered them a notice period of six months; however, feeling unsure of Robbie's commitment, the band asked him to leave sooner. He did so but not before famously asking if it was all right to take a melon with him! The break-up came during tour rehearsals and the whole show had to be rearranged to accommodate the new symmetry of the four-piece Take That.

We saw the band arrive at the Nynex but couldn't spot much through the usual blacked-out windows of their Espace – still, it was all part of the build-up. As the arena doors opened, and thousands of girls bursting with excitement made their way inside, we were almost heartbroken that we didn't have tickets. Having spent all day there, it was inconceivable that we would miss the first show. We really couldn't afford the prices the touts were charging outside and hung on at the box office until finally, and remarkably, our luck turned again and some tickets became available.

We soon swapped our positions in block D, row M to the fifth row from the stage after spotting a few girls there that we had been speaking to earlier in the day. Everyone stands up at a Take That concert so it's fairly easy to squeeze on to the ends of rows where you don't belong! All eyes were on the new four-piece Take That – could they perform as well without Robbie?

As usual they wowed their audience with elaborate dance routines and flamboyant costumes that genuinely left the girls weak at the knees and panting for breath. I was absolutely blown away by the amazing show, which always exceeds expectations. Then the moment came, 'Could It Be Magic' began and all the keen Robbie fans sensed his loss. Lisa, who was one of them, sobbed at his absence from the stage but agreed that the remaining members had done a fantastic job without him.

When the concert ends that is when the buzz is at its highest, when the appetite is most, when the desire to see them a little bit closer is strongest, and when all regular good sense seems lost in the moment. We began again at Jason's flat but there were rumours circulating that Gary was at the

Ramada hotel, drinking with one of the dancers, so we made the short trip there to check this out. According to the fans outside the hotel, Gary had been there but had left; however, a select few knew the band's hotel and, in return for this prized piece of information we offered them a lift there!

The 'Milkybar', we learned, was the Mottram Hall hotel (which was quite a way out from the centre of Manchester) and we tried to make our way there but in the days before satellite navigation it wasn't all that easy. As we got closer we noticed carloads of girls playing Take That songs, zooming around the country lanes, so we knew we were on the right track. Just before the entrance to the hotel there were a good few cars parked up at the roadside with girls sitting inside. We decided to be brave and just try to drive into the hotel, but at the top of the path that would allow this sat two burly security guys, who were not about to let anyone into the hotel who was not already a resident.

Like the others we parked up and then went to where the security guys were, around twenty girls sat huddled up on the ground in the hope that Take That would come out to say hello to them to make it all worth it. Some of the lucky few who were residents at the hotel came out to tease us with up-to-the-minute information of how the lads were drinking in the bar and holding an impromptu party. I'm sure that I would have sold one of my kidneys just to be in there too! By the early hours of the morning it was pretty clear that we were not going to see the boys and so we tried to get some sleep in the back of Lisa's car.

At dawn the security guards were gone and I walked down to the hotel to check it out. Who would have thought that walking into a hotel could be so terrifying, but there was a strong sense that I just didn't belong and was about to be found out at any moment! I'm not sure if it was because I looked as though I had slept in a car all night, but I was told by reception that there were no rooms available that evening and I'm not sure that we could have afforded it, even if there had been. We returned to the Nynex and managed once again to get last-minute tickets and enjoyed another show. As Gary ripped off his shirt and sang Nirvana's hit 'Smells Like Teen Spirit', wearing just black PVC trousers and looking incredibly fit, I couldn't help but feel let down that this hadn't turned out to be as good as before – but I wouldn't have to wait that long before I was in their presence once more.

Two weeks after the Manchester trip, JoJo and I headed to London and to Earls Court for another Take That show. At the same time Robbie was making his solo TV debut presenting on Channel 4's *The Big Breakfast*. As we had no idea where his former band mates were staying, we decided to go down to Old Ford Lock and try our luck with Robbie instead. We sat out all night by the famous white picket fence of *The Big Breakfast* house with quite a few other fans. Some had flown in from places like Italy and Denmark, and as usual to pass the time we all swapped Take That stories and talked about the band.

Crew began arriving early, followed by the show's presenters Keith Chegwin, Dani Behr – and, of course, Robbie

Williams! Between rehearsals, Robbie came over to chat to us with his mug of tea and usually a Silk Cut too; he was very cheeky and would pick out some of the prettier girls to kiss, or hold his hands up and mimic squeezing their breasts with a wide-eyed look, and of course the girls loved it. We were able to watch the show go out live on monitors placed in the garden. The outside broadcasts involved us (some two or three hundred fans) screaming away at Robbie, who did a very good job on the show, despite causing them a few headaches by changing the title of the end-of-show game 'Get Your Egg

Robbie's solo debut, presenting on Channel 4's *The Big Breakfast*.

Over' to 'Get Your Leg Over' and ruining a few microphones by jumping into the pool.

When the show finished, Robbie had to record a trailer for the following day's show and came over to stand in front of us. He was going to say, 'I'm...' then we would shout 'Robbie Williams', to which he would then say, 'And this is the...' and again we would shout 'Big Breakfast!', and finally he would say, 'Boom, boom, boom, let me hear you say Va-le,' and we shouted 'Va-le!' (as in Port Vale, his beloved football team, for any that are not in the know!).

One week after seeing Robbie at *The Big Breakfast*, we were back down in London, having discovered that Take That were once again staying at the exclusive Chelsea Harbour hotel, the Conrad. JoJo's cousin (also a big Take That fan) had booked a rather expensive room there and we arrived excitedly to check in. No sooner had we entered the plush lobby of the hotel than Gary came out from behind a pillar and walked straight past me, wearing a sleeveless white top and leaving behind a delicious waft of his aftershave. I was taken aback at how quickly we had seen one of them, as normally there is some sitting around involved.

Gary had gone to join Mark on the terrace just outside the bar to have lunch, and, after we had taken our bags up to our rather gorgeous room, we went to the bar to get a drink. We didn't speak to Gary or Mark: it was exciting enough to occasionally glance at them (not wanting to stare rudely, of course) as they enjoyed their lunch in the sunshine, and to smile at them as they walked through the bar after they had finished. We took up position in the lobby and watched them all gather to leave for the concert that evening and, as we were not going, we took a walk round the harbour and tried to get enough money together for some chips each. In fact, one of the broadsheets at the time reported how this swanky London hotel had been overrun with teenage girls eating McDonald's in their posh reception area, much to the annoyance and complaint of their more regular customers!

That evening, many of Take That's more affluent fans, who could afford to stay at the hotel, dressed to impress and filled the areas from the outside terrace into the bar and all the way through down to reception. The band would not normally come into the front of the hotel after a concert but would instead use one of the lower ground-floor entrances that linked onto the car park. They would then have time to shower and get changed from their stage clothes before coming to join their fans in the bar area. It would become clear that one or more members might be on their way as a table or two would be cleared and set aside for them by security. I'm not even sure if they had the authority to do that, but nonetheless we were not going to argue – we wanted to see them!

Tonight, sadly there were no tables cleared, no grand entrance from the boys we were all waiting for, and as it got later and later people slowly disappeared up to their rooms. I think that it was past two in the morning and JoJo and I were up in our room when suddenly we had an urge to go down one more time to take a last look round. The reception area and bar were now deserted but outside the hotel a vehicle was pulling up and a few dedicated fans that had been patiently waiting there began to move closer to it and then started to take photographs. Suddenly I became very nervous as I realised that this was the band returning to the hotel and we sat down on one of the sofas near to the glass revolving doors at the front and waited, trying to look relaxed and casual of course!

First in were Gary and Howard making their way to the bar, followed by Mark and Jason. They stood chatting but we were too far away to hear what they were saying. Just a few hours earlier, this place had been bursting at the seams with excited females but now just the two of us sat here, not quite believing our luck. Before we knew it, Gary and Howard were coming towards us and went into one of the lifts, leaving me questioning why I hadn't had the courage to at least say hello to them as they passed!

Next to walk over was Jason. 'Good evening,' he said politely, with a big smile on his face. We shyly responded with a 'Hello' and then watched as he pushed the button to call the lift. I desperately searched my brain for something to say. 'And how are we this evening?' he asked, as he waited.

'Yes, good thanks,' I managed, while silently screaming at myself to initiate some sort of better conversation, but, with nothing forthcoming, off Jason went, too.

Last came Mark, certainly looking as though he had had a fair few to drink, but now clutching a large bottle of Evian as he too headed towards the lift. JoJo's long blonde hair was hanging over the back of the sofa and Mark inadvertently touched it as he leaned his hand down and said hello to us, asking how we were.

'This time I am going to talk,' I thought, and I blurted out, 'Are you going to bed now, Mark? Because we are very tired...' Of all the possible combinations of words I had at my disposal, why did I choose that? What about asking how the tour was going or complimenting him on a great performance? Mark took a sip from his bottle of water and said that he was going to bed and then stood biting the top of the bottle while waiting for the lift. We returned to the room, and of course JoJo's cousin was gutted that she had missed everything, but not nearly as gutted as I was for not being able to speak coherently in my fortunate position of being one on one with Take That!

The next day, in the lobby of the hotel, fans gossiped, as always, about the band. This was fuelled by the fact that a couple of the dancers that were apparently supposed to be staying in a different hotel came down from the lifts with Mark, who announced to everyone that he was going shopping. Another of the rumours was about a certain Italian girl called Francesca. It seemed that everyone knew about this girl and her supposed liaisons with Gary. One story was that Gary had let her into his home at Plumley, Cheshire, in full view of other fans outside and she had also apparently told people that she had been intimate with him on several occasions. I refused to believe it and passed it off as hearsay, but, as Gary walked through the lobby that afternoon, he pulled this Francesca to one side and had a discussion with her before going back to his room.

Just before the tour started, JoJo and I had been working on putting a demo tape together and had recorded a couple of songs in a little government-run studio in Coventry. We had decided to bring this tape with us to the hotel in case we saw the band's manager Nigel Martin-Smith and could pass it to him in person. In the afternoon, Mark was walking around largely undisturbed, such was the unwritten protocol of only asking for photos and autographs outside the hotel as a vague act of respect towards the lads' privacy. I decided that, since we had not seen Nigel, I would just ask Mark to give the tape to him instead. As he passed by, I nervously said, 'Excuse me, Mark. Could you give this to your manager, please?' He paused and took the tape from me before asking me what it was. I told him it was our demo tape (pointing to JoJo); he looked puzzled, but agreed to my request. We never heard anything back so either Nigel recognised the songs for the awful dirge that they were or else Mark duly binned it once out of sight! Nothing much else happened that day, unless you count the rather peculiar decision we made to tape a sign saying 'Boo!' to the back of one of the lifts and send it up to Take That's floor for the security to have a laugh at, oh dear! Sadly, it was time to leave and await our next adventure with the boys.

3

THE SPLIT, THE BRITS
AND GOING SOLO

In February 1996, rumours circulated that our beloved Take That were to split. Though at first we were loath to believe it, confirmation came during a press conference that began with Gary's immortal words, 'Unfortunately, the rumours are true', at which millions of fans worldwide shuddered. We had already been planning to go to the Brit Awards that year, where the boys were set to perform their brand-new single 'How Deep is Your Love', and, had it not been for the *Sun* newspaper leaking it, this is where they had planned to announce that they were to part ways. Now that the Brits performance had taken on new meaning as their last-ever show in the UK, we were even more certain that we should be there.

It was absolutely freezing on the day of the Brit Awards 1996 – there were even patches of ice on the ground – but hundreds of keen Take That fans stood, as always, at the gates of Earls Court in London, with heavy hearts and wishing to say goodbye to the guys that had given them so much joy over the previous few years. JoJo and I had booked a bed and breakfast close by, and from our window we could actually see the side of the venue and Michael Jackson walking by with his entourage. This was the year that he performed 'Earth Song' and Jarvis Cocker was arrested for invading the stage during the performance!

Without tickets, we listened to the latest show information on the radio in the room and then decided to go down to try to catch Take That leaving from the back of the arena. Most of the fans were round the front so it was fairly quiet where we were, and after a while some people began leaving. In an amazing stroke of luck (ones that we were becoming accustomed to) a couple approached us and said that they were not attending the aftershow party and asked if we wanted their tickets. My God, this was amazing, a party with the boys, not to mention all of the other stars that were merrily swigging back champagne just inside the doors that we now had access to!

We raced back to the B&B (trying not to slip and break our

The lucky Brit Awards ticket, 1996.

necks on the icy road) and got changed into something slightly more appropriate for a celebrity party, with a sense of urgency and excitement to get back before Take That decided to leave. We marched past the security at Earls Court with the kind of confidence that having two golden tickets in your pocket affords and excitedly entered the world of showbiz. The party had been set up like a funfair with rides and attractions inside. Julia Carling was playing a fruit machine and Noel Gallagher passed by. We got ourselves some champagne and scoured the huge party for Gary, Mark, Jason and Howard. It felt like we were going round in circles and we were getting the sense that a lot of the A-list celebrities had moved on to other parties. We started chatting to a photographer in there, who confirmed that Take That had already gone; however, he knew the hotel where they were staying and offered us a lift there when he left. We were annoyed that we had missed them, but at least we now knew the hotel.

As promised, we took the journey with the photographer to the Athenaeum hotel in Piccadilly. Outside there were metal barriers separating two crowds of girls, who were being watched over by security. Clutching our Brits programmes and champagne flutes (trying to look as though we belonged), we walked straight between them and into the hotel, somehow managing to avoid any questions. Having never been to the hotel before, we had no idea which way to go to get to the bar and were petrified of being thrown out or interrogated by the receptionists, so we headed for the lifts and went up a few floors and then stood on the corridor, wondering what to do next.

We knew we needed to be brave but this hotel was the snootiest we'd ever been in and deathly quiet inside, no usual rabble of fans. Picturing Take That in the bar was the incentive we needed to go back down and try to look confident as we attempted to locate the bar area. Down we went and made a swift right turn out of the lifts and into an area with some tables and chairs. We were the only ones in there and too frightened to order a drink as it was past midnight and they would have needed to know a room number, which of course we did not have! After a while, we heard some noise from outside and what sounded like Mancunian accents in the lobby. Still no one entered the room we were in. Hours passed, and we had nowhere to go: if we had tried to make our way through to another bar, we might have been asked to leave and we didn't have enough money for a cab so we would have had to wait until the morning when the buses were running again!

At around 6 a.m. I ordered a pot of coffee and, as I had predicted, I was asked for my room number. I made one up, but then he asked for my name and I came clean. 'Would you like us to leave?' I asked. 'We would have liked it if you hadn't sat here all night!' came the snooty reply, to which I cheekily responded, 'Could I still have my coffee, though?' The man agreed and, as I lifted posh brown sugar lumps with equally posh silver tongs into my hot drink, I gasped at the bill I had been handed – we could have got a cab for the same amount of money!

Mark leaving the Athenaeum hotel after the Brit Awards.

We returned to the B&B to pack up and check out, and then went back to the Athenaeum to sit outside this time with at least a hundred others, waiting for the departure of the band. Many of the girls had banners saying things like 'Thank you for the best years of my life' and 'We'll "Never Forget" you' or simply 'Please come "Back for Good"'.

Mark left at around lunchtime and spent a long time talking to fans, including several in tears. He signed autographs, posed for photos and told us that Gary and Howard had not stayed there last night, but that Jason would be out soon. We waited and waited. Having had no sleep the previous night and it being freezing cold made it painful, but Jason emerged at around 4 p.m. and he too spent time with the fans before being whisked away in a chauffeur-driven Jaguar.

That was the end of Take That; although they did go on to do promotion in Europe and officially end in Amsterdam in April, we knew we would not see them again as a band. I tried to be positive – though it would not be the same, surely with several solo careers in the pipeline it would get easier to meet them?

At the Athenaeum in London, I had swapped phone numbers with a fan called Lorraine as we had got on really well. We decided to get together one day at the Grosvenor House hotel on Park Lane to try to meet Gary as he arrived to receive two prestigious Ivor Novello awards for 'Back for Good', or, as he described it on the day, 'The best fifteen minutes' work I've ever done!' Knowing that it would be hard to get into the hotel, but not wanting to waste money booking a room, we decided to reserve a table for lunch just in case we were questioned as we tried to get in.

As we parked the car, we completely missed Gary arriving with his girlfriend, Dawn, and former band mate Howard, and, since they left later from the back of the hotel, we missed that too! One thing had come from the day: a great new friend and partner-in-crime in the quest to meet the artists formerly known as Take That. I would soon be frequently making the trip down to London to see the boys as they launched their solo careers.

The first of these opportunities came from Mark, who in June 1996 was at the BBC studios in Elstree to present *Top of the Pops*. One good thing about being at Elstree is that it is also where *EastEnders* is filmed so the long hours waiting were eased by spotting members of the cast as they arrived and left the building. Mark had drawn a particularly large crowd on this gloriously sunny day and he took time to come and see his fans in the afternoon after rehearsals had taken place.

We didn't have tickets to go inside and so we waited in a car opposite the exit to the studios with several others doing the same and watched for Mark's car to leave. When he finally pulled out of the gates, engines started and cars furiously sped off behind him; girls shouted angrily from car windows as everyone was trying to get out on to the main road at the same time. Off we went, position number four in a ten-car chase of poor old Mark Owen!

His chauffeur would try to trick us by indicating left when in fact they were to turn right, or by going round a roundabout a few times to try to create confusion. After about fifteen minutes, there were still a good six cars that had managed to keep up and it seemed we were driving all through London, not knowing where we were headed, but still desperate to stay behind Mark's car. It was a fine line between being close enough to follow and not so close that Mark would recognise you in a hotel at a later date as 'those girls' that had given him such grief!

When we were down to about four cars, Mark pulled over to the roadside and we all did the same, pulling in behind him. His chauffeur came over to each car in turn – we were in second place at this point – and asked us if we would please stop following. As we passed his now stationary car, Mark had the window open and was smiling and waving. What a nice guy! I think anyone else would have been screaming and shouting abuse at the inconvenience.

Two weeks later and it was back down to London once more, this time with a dual purpose. I had decided to move there and wanted to look at flats, but it was also Robbie's 'Freedom' press conference. Having been tied into a recording contract with RCA but seeing that they would give priority to Gary's solo career, Robbie had wanted out for some time. That evening at midnight he was holding a press conference to celebrate his freedom, announce his new record deal with EMI and launch his first solo single, 'Freedom', a cover version of George Michael's hit. We sat as usual in the lobby of the hotel where the press conference was taking place and told staff that we were waiting to be picked up by an uncle. Robbie arrived, wearing an England football shirt, and he looked miserable as he shared the country's pain at Gareth Southgate's missed penalty against Germany that had just seen us out of Euro '96. Robbie had been at the game and was expressing how gutted he felt.

He disappeared downstairs for the press conference and we waited in the lobby for him to leave. The night dragged on and I spoke to a journalist who told me that Robbie was doing interviews all night in a room upstairs and that his slot to speak to him was at around 4 a.m. I asked if he would he able

Gary at Elstree studios for his solo debut on *Top of the Pops*.

to get me in, saying that I was his assistant or something, and he agreed to it. Up we went in the lift, only to be told that Robbie was too tired now and was not doing any more interviews because he was live on *The Big Breakfast* in just a couple of hours and needed to rest – oh so close!

Another night of no sleep and there we were, having some tea and watching *The Big Breakfast* in the hotel bar. Lorraine went to the toilet and, when she returned, she told us that she had just seen Robbie leaving the hotel. We kept watching the show and, sure enough, there he was being interviewed live from another location in London. Well, as England had also learned the previous night, you can't win them all!

Over the next few weeks, I was down in London again, sorting out my new flat just a few streets from where Lorraine lived and going to see Gary as he promoted his first-ever solo single 'Forever Love'. We waited at the *Top of the Pops* studios again with several hundred others and cringed as they attempted to sing Gary's beautiful new song at him in a range of varying keys, none of which seemed quite right! We pursued his car as he left, but soon lost him. Days later we pulled up at BBC TV Centre just in time to see him signing some autographs before his appearance on the *National Lottery Show*.

At the same time Robbie was out promoting his first solo single 'Freedom' and this meant another trip to *Top of the Pops* to try to catch him. Lorraine's work commitments meant that we could not spend the whole day at the studios but we arrived late to give chase to his car. We lost him somewhere in

Maida Vale but soon spotted some activity on a nearby road. All the signs were there – cars containing girls and some standing outside, talking excitedly as though something great had just happened. Then we saw the car that we had been following drive away from 42 Randolph Avenue – we had found Robbie's flat!

Two days later we decided to drive over to Robbie's abode as the tabloids were reporting that he had been seen drinking in his local pub. With no sign of him there, we waited near his flat and soon spotted him walking the short journey from the off-licence round the corner to his home. It was horrible at the time for the fans to see what was happening to Robbie: it was widely reported that he was having problems in his career, as well as with his weight, and was drinking heavily. We had grown attached to these people and couldn't help but care about them. In a sense we all wanted to help, but we knew it was not our place. There were just a million things that I wanted to say to him, but how could I be any more than just a fan? Modern society has created this strange situation where we the spectators feel as though we know the people splashed across our media every day. To them, however, we are just strangers.

It wasn't as if Robbie was always alone when we saw him, though. There were other times when he was with his girlfriend Jacqui Hamilton-Smith (who lived near him) and also some of his friends. One evening as we were drinking in the local pub we saw Robbie – wearing khaki jeans and a white jacket – walk past with Jacqui. She went to her home and

The first of many...Gary and Lorraine, Ealing 1996.

Robbie, with his friends, headed for a wine bar at the top of the road. We were walking towards the wine bar but Robbie left and attempted to hail a cab; unsuccessful, they all returned to his flat and we went home.

The next day I made a quick jaunt over there again and there were about ten girls outside his flat, watching a black Jeep Cherokee being loaded up with his belongings for a promotional trip. He left, wearing a blue Adidas tracksuit, and stopped for a moment to speak to his fans. I didn't like spending too much time at the flat (tempting as it was, being so near) – but, if you're going for a drink, why not pick the same pub that Robbie Williams drinks in?

Towards the end of August I received a telephone call from Lorraine to say that Gary was recording a TV show that evening in Ealing. We made it over to the White House studios, where *The White Room* was being filmed for Channel 4. Gary was to perform a version of Roachford's 'Cuddly Toy' and his very own number-one hit, 'Forever Love'. We hadn't been there long when out walked Gary with three other men and we were quite stunned to see the four of them walk across the park, laughing and joking, when we had been so used to seeing them only with security or being whisked away in cars with blacked-out windows.

We followed at a distance and saw them enter a Chinese restaurant. And so we waited in the park, hoping to catch them as they returned to the studio. We didn't want to go inside the restaurant as we thought Gary wouldn't have been too happy with that! After a good hour and a half, out came

Gary, who crossed the road and headed straight for us. I was nervous as hell, almost shaking, but I knew I couldn't let another opportunity pass me by – I *had* to speak to him this time! 'Excuse me, Gary,' I began, 'could we have our picture taken with you?'

He smiled and said, 'Of course you can.'

We moved side by side and Gary put his arm around my shoulder while Lorraine took the picture and then we swapped. 'Thank you, Gary, see you later!' I managed, my head buzzing.

'See you later!' he replied, walking off back to the studio.

Everyone had a favourite in Take That and Gary was most definitely mine, so this was a moment I had been waiting to have for some time. I called JoJo back in Coventry to tell her what had just happened and how lovely Gary had been, and she was really thrilled. We stayed on until after the show and, when Gary drove out, he stopped the car and – I think because it might have been raining a little bit – he let the other girls who were waiting for him sit on his lap in the back of the car to have their pictures taken too.

In my happiness brought about by the evening's events, I hadn't realised that the shot of the drug that I was addicted to had just been upped, and the bigger the dose, the greater the craving...

4

ABBEY ROAD

On 4 September 1996, soon after Mark began recording his first solo album *Green Man* there, I made my way down to the famous Abbey Road studios in London. Some friends of mine had been there a few nights before and had had a chat with Mark on the steps outside, so we pulled up in a car and kept watch for a possible repeat performance. A few hours went by and nothing really seemed to be happening, except the security guy (who some other girls were relentlessly pestering for information) seemed to be quite a friendly chap.

I decided to go into the studios and speak to him. At first I asked if I could use the toilet and he asked why I hadn't gone before I left my house, so I began spinning some yarn about how I had been close by visiting a friend and how I was waiting for someone to pick me up, and so on. After we had been chatting for a while, the other group of girls came and started knocking on the door so the security guy (who I now knew as

Behind the desk at Abbey Road Studios.

Bob) told me to sit down behind the desk with him, which I did. The girls were asking, 'Is Mark coming out tonight?' and Bob responded that he didn't know and he laughed.

As we were chatting, my friend called me from outside to find out what was going on; she had work the next morning and was keen to go home. Bob said he could get me a taxi later, paid for by the studios, so my friend left and I stayed. I chatted to him about the studios and couldn't believe my luck that a simple request to use the loo had turned into access to arguably the most famous recording studios in the world!

As the night drew on, all of the girls went home, and then

out from a nearby studio door walked Mark! He came over to Bob and me and asked if he could borrow £3 for the cigarette machine (those were the days!). I reached for my bag and told him that he could borrow the money. He thanked me and then said that he would pay me back the next time he saw me. I argued that he wouldn't be seeing me again, but, as he had assumed that I must work there, he didn't understand this and frowned. Nonetheless, off he went, leaving behind a strong smell of patchouli oil as he did. I think he was going through his hippie phase! As always, he looked absolutely beautiful – stunning blue eyes and soft brown skin, with a calm, sweet and very polite nature. It is easy to see why so many girls fell in love with him.

Once Mark had finished for the night, Bob had to go round and lock everything up and he left me waiting behind the desk. When he returned, he told me that Mark was outside alone. My heart pounded: whenever in this world do you get an opportunity like that? I couldn't resist, so I walked outside and towards Mark, who was indeed alone and smoking a cigarette while reading some of the graffiti that the fans had left for him on the famous Abbey Road wall. I said, 'Hey there,' and he responded with a 'Y'all right?' in his husky Northern tones.

One of the messages on the wall read: 'Alex, you are the best manager in the world', in reference to his then manager Alex Kadis. I asked him if he had written that one but he laughed and shook his head. We chatted and laughed at some of the other messages and I asked him if it was weird having so many girls waiting outside for him; he said yes but that it was also nice to have some peace as his life had been very hectic. I apologised for disturbing his peace but he said, 'No, you're all right.' Nonetheless, I felt that I should go, so I wished him goodnight and went back inside the studio.

As promised, Bob called me a cab and, as I got into it, I saw that Mark was sitting on the steps to the building next door (which was in fact Abbey Road's garden flat, where he was staying at the time) and he waved at me and shouted goodbye with a beaming smile – he really is as nice as he seems on TV.

A few days later I received a call from Bob saying that he was working at Abbey Road that night and asking if I wanted to go along. Without hesitation, I got the tube and waited at a nearby bus stop until it was clear for me to enter. I had a lot of fun that night: Bob let me answer the phones and at one point I received a call from Mark's girlfriend at the time, Joanna Kelly, but I couldn't transfer the call as he was already on the line to his manager. Bob told me that in this instance I would have to go to the studio and tell Mark that he had a call. I knocked on the door and then opened it: Mark was sitting on the sofa with the phone to his ear and he looked at me. I told him that Joanna was on the other line and he smiled and put his thumb up before I turned and closed the door.

I didn't see him again on this occasion but, after he had gone to bed, Bob took me into his studio and played me what was to become Mark's first single 'Child'. It sounded so beautiful and so amazing that I cried, but of course I would never be able to tell Mark what I had thought of it! Despite the fact that I never screamed or asked for an autograph or anything like that (in fact, I was there in times of cigarette withdrawal), I do feel guilty that I was in Mark's space in such a way but I was very young and the temptation proved too much. Mark, please forgive me and, hey, don't worry about that £3!

At the time he was recording his solo debut at Abbey Road, Robbie continued to live close by on Randolph Avenue. We had still never really spoken to him, but when we did see him pass by sometimes we smiled at each other – he probably

In Mark's studio, where I listened to 'Child'.

thought we lived nearby! One evening, after learning from Bob that Robbie had been to visit Mark at Abbey Road all day and that they had gone out, we went down to Maida Vale to see if they were in any of the bars. With no luck, we were walking back to the car and had just passed Rob's flat when we heard some guys behind shout something at us. Thinking it was a couple of drunken yobs, I yelled, 'Get lost!' and carried on walking. My friend turned to look at the people who had shouted and quickly informed me that I had just told Robbie and Mark where to go. Not believing her, I spun round and, sure enough, there they were, going down the steps to Robbie's basement flat. Who knows what they wanted or what could have happened had I not been so rude? Needless to say, regret has haunted me ever since!

I went to Abbey Road a few more times before Mark left. One evening, as I arrived, he was in reception with Joanna and their new black puppy dog, which I think was named Cosmic or Cosmos! Mark even left a message with Bob on his final day to say thanks and goodbye to me. Shortly after he had gone, a large party was thrown at Abbey Road, called 'The Gathering'. It was rumoured that Paul McCartney was going to attend and obviously I hoped Mark would be there too.

Huge spotlights and paparazzi greeted us as we arrived and I helped myself to plenty of free drinks inside and got chatting to a few people, one of whom was David Macintosh, an American music producer. That evening he was staying in the garden flat (which Mark had just vacated) and invited me and some others down there to continue the party. I was

CLEMENTINE

She heard a voice from so faraway
It told her her mother had gone away
In the next room down the corridor
Her baby started to cry
Her whole life had just fell apart
There was nothing then the hurting started
In her heavy head on her knees she prayed
Could somebody help her

CHORUS

Clementine
It was never meant to be this way
It was never meant to be this way
Clementine
It was never meant to be this way
It was never meant to be this way
~~For the child~~
~~For the mother~~   If only I had told you yesterday.
~~Could we help her~~

Got in her car and she sped away
Into the floodlit street down by your way
As the sun rose through the morning dew
She returned in such a state
Her baby knew not what was going on
But it could tell from the tears somethings wrong with mum
Desperation let out it's final scream
But our Clementine she didn't hear a damn thing

CHORUS

Clementine
It was never meant to be this way
It was never meant to be this way
Clementine
It was never meant to be this way
It was never meant to be this way
~~For the child~~
~~For the mother~~   If only I had told you yesterday
~~Could we help her~~

Into the mirror she stared at herself
Asked is this my life is this what i'm here for
Her reflection chose not to responde
So she froze to the spot like a cold stone statue
Bathed in her tears said her time was through

Mark's corrected lyric sheets.

really excited to look around the flat that had very recently been Mark's home and took myself on a tour. I looked into the bedroom and was thinking of how Mark had been sleeping there just a few nights previously when David joined me and said, 'Yeah, amazing, isn't it? This is where John Lennon and Yoko Ono stayed.' Of course I wasn't going to let on that I had, in fact, been thinking of Mark Owen! A little later on, we all climbed out of the window and I saw the steps that Mark had been sitting on the night he waved goodbye to me, and we took some very silly drunken photos holding pieces of furniture from the famous garden flat on the famous zebra crossing!

5

MORE SOLO ADVENTURES

With three solo careers on the go, it was proving to be quite a fun time in our adventures with Gary, Mark and Robbie, and now that I lived in London it wasn't much of a hardship getting around to see them. Gary had scored his first solo number one with 'Forever Love', and Robbie (although outselling Gary by 40,000 copies) had gone in at number two, only missing out on the coveted top spot thanks to a certain new girl band called the Spice Girls. Mark followed the trend by reaching number three with his song 'Child'.

With their continuing success, 1997 looked as though it was going to be a busy year for us too, the devoted fans! In February we followed Mark from the *Top of the Pops* studios in Elstree once more, but this time in the afternoon to the Moat House hotel nearby. We waited outside, and in one of the rooms above we saw relentless camera flashes and assumed he must have gone there for a photo shoot. When he left, Lorraine had her picture taken with him, but I stood by the car, hiding behind my video camera, as I did not want Mark to recognise me from Abbey Road and realise what I had done!

I was still friends with Bob from Abbey Road – although now he was Bob from the equally prestigious Townhouse studios in West London. One evening, he called to tell me that Elton John was recording there, whom he said had invited him to his 50th birthday bash at the Hammersmith Palais that April, and that I could be his 'plus one'. I was really excited and looked

Lorraine and Mark at the Moat House hotel, London in February 1997.

forward to it immensely, especially since Gary was expected to attend. Sadly, just before the event, Bob revealed that he had been pressured into taking his sister, but I decided to go down to the party anyway to watch the arrivals and maybe try to get Bob to sneak me in a bit later.

There were lots of stars arriving at the extravagant event and all of them in fancy dress! Lenny Henry and Dawn French (who was a teddy bear), Des O'Connor and his girlfriend Jodie in matching cowgirl and cowboy outfits, and the man of the moment, Sir Elton, in a Louis XIV wig so high he had to use a furniture van as his transport for the evening!

Then, to my utter frustration (at the party I had thought that I would be going to), out stepped Gary, Howard *and* Jason, posing for photographers before making their way inside. Howard was dressed as Batman, Gary as Robin (with his girlfriend, Dawn, as Catwoman) and Jason was the Riddler! I tried and failed to get through to Bob on his mobile, so I gave up and took a cab home.

My luck would return soon, though, when I was invited, with Lorraine and a few others, on to a new ITV show called *The Funky Bunker*, presented by Craig Charles. They requested audience members dress space age and so, not wanting to disappoint, we went all out, with wigs, silver eyeliner and matching lipstick. We were spotted in the queue and congratulated on the effort we had made; as such, we were to have prime positions around the bar where Craig would be presenting the show. We got chatting to a guy who worked on the show and it turned out that he was in charge of recruiting audiences for a great variety of TV shows including *TFI Friday*, *CD:UK* and *The Pepsi Chart Show*.

As he had been so impressed by us, he gave us his number and told us that he could put us on the guest lists for any of the shows that he dealt with, if we just gave him a call. This was great news! Trying to get TV show tickets can be a tricky business, especially for the popular ones as they can have long waiting lists. It is also hard to get the timing right – you can apply for tickets fairly easily but you may not end up with tickets for the day when the artist you want to see is performing. This was going to make our lives a lot easier and it wasn't long before we took up his offer, as a few days later Robbie was performing on *TFI Friday* to promote his new single 'Old Before I Die'.

Bypassing the long queue of people waiting to get into the studio, we checked our names on the guest list and went inside to have a drink before the show began. Robbie was interviewed by host of the show Chris Evans, before making his way through the crowd to join his band on stage and sing his new song. He very amusingly changed one line in the song to 'I hope I live to receive Channel Five', which had launched recently and was having a few problems!

After the song had finished, Robbie sat at the base of the drum kit and we were close by, at the front of the stage. He was waiting to do some more recording for some trailers for the show and for a section called 'It's your letters', when I noticed that not all seemed to be well with the Robster. He seemed confused and appeared to be chattering to himself; it looked as if he was on drugs. He also seemed to have lost a lot of confidence, although he managed to cover this with humour. It was really sad for me to see Robbie like that; he made eye contact at one point and I smiled at him and he smiled back, but, really, I just wanted to give him a big hug. My time was coming!

Five days after the *TFI* recording, I was at the BBC TV studios at Wood Lane for the recording of the *National Lottery Show*, where Robbie's now arch-rival Gary was to perform his next single 'Love Won't Wait'. I had been given a spare ticket by a fan that I got talking to outside and now I was queuing with her and other audience members when I noticed that Gary had gone down to see the crowd at the main gates. I lost my place in the queue to go out on to a balcony in an attempt to intercept him on his way back into the building, all the while mindful of being stopped by security and hauled off the premises. My plan worked and, as Gary approached, I managed to stop him for a moment. I told him that I had been at the party the other night and had seen his Robin costume, which made him laugh; I also wished him success with his single.

The following month I was on holiday in Ibiza and had to rely on Lorraine to fill me in on the comings and goings of the Prince's Trust concert up in Manchester, where Gary was to perform his next song 'So Help Me Girl'. She had tracked him down to the luxury Midland hotel but, although she had seen him a few times, she had not spoken to him. The Spice Girls were also staying at the hotel, as was Jennifer Aniston, all there to make appearances at the Prince's Trust concert. While sitting in the lobby, *Friends* star Jennifer came over to ask Lorraine why so many girls were there. Lorraine pointed out Gary, explaining that he was the reason why. 'Oh, he is very gorgeous,' she agreed. 'I can see why!'

On my return from holiday, we were off to the Soccer Six tournament in Fulham, London. This annual charity event involved several celebrity football teams, all playing quick-fire five-a-side matches until the winning team was awarded a trophy at the end. Players in previous years included Noel and Liam Gallagher and this year featured Damon Albarn, Jamie Theakston, the Prodigy, the Stereophonics and the guys that I had gone to support: Robbie Williams and Mark Owen.

Not having seen the boys together since Robbie left the band back in 1995, it was nice to see them in the sunshine, sitting on the grass and chatting in between games – even laughing hysterically when a female streaker ran across the pitch near them! It wasn't all smiles for Robbie, though, and, as he made his way back and forth from the game to the changing rooms, he looked sad and swigged on pints of beer before going back out to the public and mooning them before his next match.

A few weeks later, on 6 July, it was not a member of Take That, but rather their former rivals East 17, who was about to make a somewhat embarrassing appearance in my life. Lorraine and I had been in the nightclub Charlie Chan's and were excited to see the very handsome David Beckham enter and join us at the bar. He didn't seem to be interested in any

Robbie looking unhappy at the Soccer Six event.

of the girls like the other footballers were; he looked distant and miserable, and, having just begun his relationship with Victoria, he was no doubt missing her.

Later, when Lorraine and I left, we spotted him driving in a convertible with the roof down, despite it being past midnight. We decided to see where he was going. Having just lost him, we ended up in Walthamstow and spotted Brian Harvey outside a kebab shop there.

We were at traffic lights when he came over to our car and told us to turn around and park in the car park opposite. Intrigued, we did so, and he came over to us, munching on his kebab. At first we pretended that we didn't know who he was and asked his name, which we thought would wind him up, but soon he was asking us what we were up to for the rest of the evening. We told him that we were just on our way home and he asked if he could join us. Thinking it might be quite fun to chat to him about his days in the pop charts, we agreed and he gave us a nearby meeting place as he was going to get his friend and his car.

We waited there for a while and then Brian and his friend pulled up and he opened his window to speak to us. He was asking if I had any alcohol at my flat because he didn't have any – all he had left was one can of Special Brew! Unfortunately I didn't, but we went to my place anyway. Just as we were walking up the road towards my flat, I suddenly realised that I had a few pictures of Take That around: I had framed the one of Gary and I taken in Ealing and there were a few pictures of Mark and Robbie around too.

Once inside, I jokingly apologised and turned the picture over, but he said that Take That were actually really cool guys and most of the rivalry between them had been orchestrated by the press. Then he spotted my collection of old *Smash Hits* magazines and started to go through them, spotting some articles and pictures of himself and his former band. I got out my video camera to make a little video of my famous guest, but he hid his face behind a magazine. We sat around chatting and I even dug out my old demo tape and played it to him. He said that I should release it in Japan and it would make a killing – I've never quite understood whether this was a compliment or not! After a while he left, but not before taking Lorraine's number – although we never did hear from him again.

A couple of weeks later, Lorraine and I decided to go up to Manchester for the weekend and she offered to show me Gary's old house in Plumley, Cheshire. It was located next door to a pub that doubled as a bed and breakfast, so we decided to stay there. In the Take That days, the place used to be full of fans, eager to see Gary at his home, and the rooms overlooking his house were especially popular as was the car park outside, where fans would sleep in their cars.

Gary had gone on to sell this house to Jason Orange and, despite the band having split more than a year earlier, there were still a fair few girls around. We got talking to some that were parked up and they had somehow got hold of a couple of Howard's songs that he had recorded in a bid to launch his own solo career. I absolutely loved 'Speak Without Words' and it's a real shame that he never got the chance to enjoy success with it. They also had some of Robbie's unreleased songs on tape and it was becoming clear to me that, despite everybody commenting on how Gary was the next George Michael, Robbie was also going to be one to watch.

The following day we were sunbathing (as you do) on the grass outside what was now Jason Orange's home when the gates opened and there he stood, wearing a pair of shorts and a T-shirt. 'Oh no!' he began. 'Now you are all going to see my skinny legs!'

Despite our reassurances that he had nothing to worry

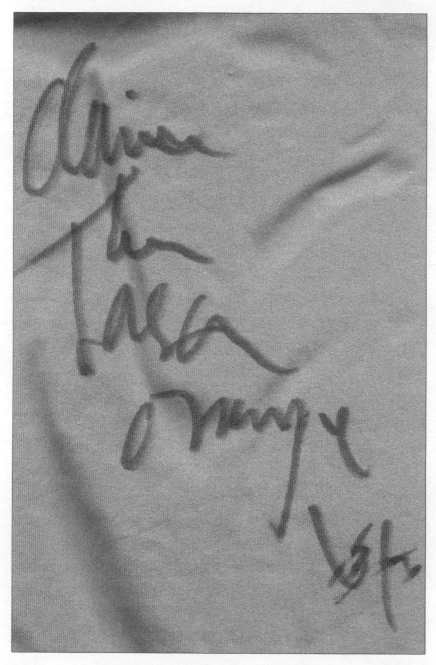

The blue top signed by Jason Orange.

about, he seemed genuinely embarrassed. In all, there were about ten of us there and Jason was happy to sign autographs and chat for a while. As I had no paper, I asked him to sign the back of my top, but he was concerned that this would destroy it – which is strange logic, considering that it would have actually added value should I have later decided to sell it on eBay for example!

He also made the rather terse comment that I would be better off getting Gary's autograph, as it would be worth more, which struck us all as a bit odd since there seemed to be some tension behind the statement. After signing my top, 'Claire, love Jason Orange xx', he turned to Lorraine and said, 'Now, would you like me to ruin your pretty little dress?'

Lorraine responded, 'No, thank you, it's brand new!'

After that, we decided the job was done and that we should go home, but we made a small detour to Cuddington Lane as this was where Gary's new mansion, Delamere Manor, was situated. There was graffiti on the road signs at the top of the road and on wooden fences nearby. Friends of ours had met Gary at his house and reported that he was very friendly and had posed for pictures with them, but I didn't want to stay. Gary meant much more to me than Jason did and I was concerned about how he would perceive me, and therefore sitting outside of his house was not something I wanted him to see me doing. Instead, we kept on driving and returned home to London.

6
MEETING JEZ

It was the end of July 1997 and Robbie was hitting the headlines again, this time with his court case against his former manager Nigel Martin-Smith, which was taking place at the High Court in London. We found out that the public were allowed into all 88 courtrooms, though the judge would not suffer any disturbances. To have a chance of getting in, we needed to get there very early to queue and so we took the first available tubes that were running that morning.

After hours of waiting, we managed to secure a place and went inside to enter Court 17. We had to admit that this was the strangest place that we had ever met one of the lads – it certainly was an experience! Most of the proceedings were incredibly boring, with lawyers spilling out incomprehensible legal jargon at each other, but there were some funnier moments as the judge tried to understand certain aspects of the boy band he had probably never heard of.

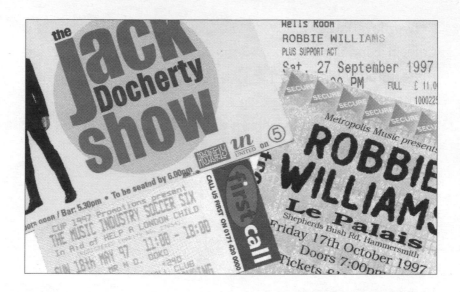

During a break we came across Robbie in the hallway and he was looking understandably sad. We spoke to him about the case and it was clear that he was under a lot of stress. There were some other fans walking along the corridor and Robbie began to cry. 'I don't want you all to see me like this,' he said.

I told him that we were there for him, no matter what, but he repeated that he just didn't want his fans to see him like that and that he wanted to show us all what he could really do. I told him that I had heard some of his songs up in Manchester and that they were really good and he thanked me. I rubbed his arm and gave him a hug, saying, 'Everything will be all right for you.' I was so relieved that I had finally managed to convey my message of care to Robbie as I had seen him so many times recently looking so terrible and I had just wanted that one opportunity to reach out to him to offer a bit of support.

Two days later, Rob was due on a TV show at the Capital Café in London's Leicester Square and so we headed down there after work for a drink and to see if we could have a chance to say hello to him again. On arrival, we spotted him hanging out of a window high above the café entrance, waving and shouting to a group of fans gathered below, and, in stark contrast to the other day at the High Court, Robbie now seemed happy and on top form.

We had heard from fellow fans during the long chats that keep you amused in the wait to see the band that Robbie could be very unpredictable in his behaviour. One evening he had been so rude to a group of girls outside a hotel that one of them shouted angrily that she had paid for the shirt he was wearing (by way of record sales). Robbie then proceeded to remove his shirt and throw it at her! Then, at other times, he would spend a long time with his fans chatting and being really nice. This erratic behaviour, he claimed in one of his books released years later, was the fault of his ongoing drug use.

From Robbie's High Court battle with Nigel Martin-Smith – note the spelling mistake!

COURT 17
Before MR JUSTICE FERRIS
Thursday, 24th July, 1997
At half past 10
WITNESS LIST PART 1
WL332/96   Martin-Smith v Willaims. Action Pt Hd

While we waited around the back of the building for Robbie to leave, we spotted something very familiar to us: a shiny black Mercedes with the registration plate P571 CAN. This was the car that we had seen Gary using at various TV promotions but could he, too, really be here on this fine summer's evening?

We stood near to the car until the chauffeur returned and got into the driving seat. I walked over to the window and tapped on it. 'Hi, sorry to bother you, but do you sometimes drive Gary Barlow?' I asked. On questioning, I explained that I had seen Gary being driven into some TV studios in the same car very recently. The chauffeur admitted that he drove many stars including Gary and that on this evening he was waiting for a call from a different celebrity (but not Robbie) to go and pick him up from a nearby club. He got out of the car and I introduced him to Lorraine and he told us that his name was Jez.

We were keen to keep him chatting as we realised that he could well come in handy in the future for providing information on the whereabouts of Mr Barlow. In the end we swapped phone numbers and he said that he might be able to help us if anything came up. We thanked him and then went to wait for Robbie, who was soon to emerge with his own chauffeur and set off on to the busy London streets. His car was going so slowly that all of us managed to keep up with it on foot and there were a good fifty or sixty girls, all shouting and taking photographs. Robbie kept turning towards us, waving and smiling, and jokingly sticking his two fingers up at a paparazzo who was also there trying to take his picture.

By this time, Robbie had moved into his new top-floor flat in Pembridge Crescent, Notting Hill Gate. We had found out the location of his new pad inadvertently when the local evening news had shown Robbie emerging from the front steps on the way to rehab. He told the assembled press that he was very disappointed with the turnout – when Michael Barrymore had had his much-publicised problems, he had received far more attention! As they pushed him for information about his health, Robbie repeated that his new single 'Lazy Days' would be out soon and that things were very much business as usual.

A few weeks later, we went to his new flat to have a look and as usual there were girls waiting outside. There was also a man there, asking if any of us had Robbie's number. He claimed that he had met Robbie in rehab recently and wanted to see him again. As we were leaving, he asked us for a lift and we agreed. Once in the car, he offered us a drink of lemonade from the bottle he had been carrying, but when I took a swig it tasted like pure vodka. I hoped the rehab centre would have a more long-lasting effect on Robbie!

At the beginning of August, we received a phone call from our new chauffeur friend Jez, inviting us out for a meal at Planet Hollywood. We met in the West End of London and were impressed that we were able to queue-jump and get good seats in the restaurant. Inside, we enjoyed listening to his stories of the different celebrities that he had driven around and we tried to get the gossip on Gary from him. Of course, Lorraine and I were worried about Jez's motives: why was this guy bothering to take us out? What did he want? Not once, however, did he ever make us feel uncomfortable or make sexual advances towards either of us.

As the night progressed, Jez offered us a lift home and we walked to the car. Now call me sad if you like, but, having seen Gary Barlow being driven around in this plush, top-of-the-range Mercedes on several occasions and even chasing it full speed through London, I was really bloody excited to get inside the thing! It was so comfortable and I loved looking out of the blackened windows, knowing that people could not see in. I remembered the night at *The White Room*, where Gary had sat in this very seat, having his picture taken with his fans, and how once I had jokingly asked him for a lift as the rain started to fall. Now I was being driven home in the car and I adored every single minute of it!

Less than a week later, it was back into the West End (I told you it was a busy year!) as we had scored two tickets to a recording of *The Jack Docherty Show* and Mark was scheduled to perform. As usual, we turned up early to take up position outside the studio to get good seats at the front of the show and also to see Mark. There were a good twenty of us outside when Mark came out of a side door to say hello. He said that he was going for a walk up the road and he asked us not to follow him. But he posed for some pictures and then off he went with some of his team and we respected his wishes by awaiting his return to the studio.

The very next day, we were off to Uri Geller's house, where *The Weekend Show* was being broadcast live, with guests that included Mark Owen and Dannii Minogue. We waited by a canal running at the back of the house by a gate that seemed to provide the makeshift entrance for the guests and crew of the show. We spoke to Dannii (who was very friendly) as she made her way on to a boat to record a piece, and we could make out a small amount of the proceedings through the gate, as it was largely left open.

At some point in the afternoon, Uri Geller came out to speak to us. We thought he was going to tell us off for being too close to his property but instead he told us that he had sensed psychically that we wanted to be inside his house! Blown away by his supernatural powers (chuckle), we gratefully accepted the invitation and entered his back garden. We saw a helicopter come in to land and of course we had plenty of opportunity to speak to Mark, who was hanging around in between rehearsals and running scared from incoming wasp attacks.

One of the highlights of the show was Uri replicating a picture that Mark had previously drawn that day and kept sealed in his pocket. Uri was spot on and so I asked Mark if it was a stunt, but he swore it had been genuine. I also asked Mark for an autograph – I'm not that into them actually, but we had so much time with him that day that I thought, 'Why not?' I took my Radiohead album out from my bag, the fantastic *OK Computer* that had not long been out, and handed it to Mark along with a pen.

'I wish!' he said, staring wistfully at the cover.

'You can sign his name if you want!' I replied, but instead he scrawled just inside on the booklet: 'Ace, love Mark Owen x' – incidentally with the same pen with which he hadn't been able to sign my jeans all those years ago at the Copthorne! Mark showed no signs of recognising me from Abbey Road; nearly a year had passed and it seemed that I would no longer feel I had to hide when I saw him, which was a relief.

Two days after the visit to Uri's house and largely egged on by one of Mark's biggest fans, Claudia, who had come down from Scotland and was staying with Lorraine, we went to Southampton to see Mark perform at a radio road show.

Mark with Uri Geller.

Claudia had gone so far as to have a tattoo of a green alien on her upper arm to coincide with the title of Mark's album *Green Man* and I asked her if she didn't think that one day she would regret it. She insisted Mark would always be a part of her life and her history and, as such, the tattoo would just serve as a reminder of this.

In Southampton, we found out that Mark was staying at the Grand Harbour hotel (by doing a reservation check on his manager) and when we arrived he was in the restaurant area, having something to eat. When he walked into the foyer to leave, we stopped him for a chat and had some photos taken with him before making the short journey to the seafront, where the road show was taking place.

Next, we were off once more to the *Top of the Pops* studios in Elstree, where Mark was to perform 'I Am What I Am' – except that this time, lo and behold, we had tickets! After all that time spent hanging around outside, finally we could get in! Leaving behind the massive crowd that had come to see Mark, we went into the building. On gaining entry to the studio area, where there were several stages set up, we tried to figure out which one was Mark's to take up prime front-row positions. The producers, of course, had other ideas and kept telling us that we had to stand by another stage for a different band, so we tried to hang at the back of the crowd ready to run if they said Mark was performing next. I never understood why they just didn't record Mark first – then they wouldn't have had to struggle so hard to keep us all in line!

Dannii Minogue was there again, and she recognised us

from Uri Geller's house and waved, and then came the moment and a mad dash was made to the stage where Mark was to come out and sing. I made it to about second row, which wasn't too bad given the crush of girls aiming for this tiny bit of space in a deceptively small studio. Out came Mark and everybody was screaming and shouting his name as per usual and then he began to sing his song. Not long in, he looked at me and I smiled; then he looked again and again, until I was getting a bit freaked out. I stopped dancing and was really confused as to why Mark was looking so much. When I got home and watched the show the next evening, I could see that he is distracted by something to his left, but being there in the audience it was just so much more blatant and weird. This was definitely not an 'I recognise you' smile – in fact, it wasn't a smile at all. Perhaps he suddenly realised that I was the girl from Abbey Road and that the security that he had thanked there before he left had actually done a rather poor job of keeping fans out!

A mere ten days after the strange *Top of the Pops* experience and the whole country was experiencing a very weird and distressing time, waking up to the news that the Princess of Wales had died overnight in a car crash in Paris. Lorraine queued for hours to sign the Book of Condolence and I went to Kensington Palace to lay some flowers. It was an unbelievable experience, the sweet smell of bouquet upon bouquet hung in the air, and despite the number of people it was serenely quiet and peaceful. I walked by Harrods shortly afterwards and Mohamed Al Fayed was there, shaking hands with people and crying; it was very moving.

Mark with his adoring fans at *Top of the Pops*, 1997.

On the day of the funeral, we made our way up to Glasgow for a Wet Wet Wet concert that was happening the following day with Mark as the support act. One of my friends had managed to blag us some backstage passes so we were especially excited. We stayed at a gorgeous hotel overnight and even hired a limo as a special treat to take us to the Celtic football ground where the concert was taking place. As promised, we were issued with wristbands that allowed us access to the backstage area, although it wasn't really that glamorous, just a few Portakabins. We saw Mark in one of them with his girlfriend, and as such we didn't bother them.

Instead, we went up to the bar and enjoyed some drinks. When Mark introduced his song 'Child', he dedicated it to Diana and changed the first line of the second verse from 'Hero, now that you are free' to 'Lady, now that you are free', which left us all with tears in our eyes.

Around the same time as Mark's promotional tour for 'I Am What I Am', Lorraine and I received a call from chauffeur Jez, who was driving the American actor Kevin Spacey. He said that Kevin was looking for some company that evening and asked if we wanted to go and join him? Well, we had just seen a certain little film called *Seven* (in which Spacey plays a psychopathic serial killer) and there was absolutely no way we wanted to go and hang out with *that* guy! We politely refused, but it turned out to be yet another of those desperate regrets. After seeing his performance in *American Beauty* in 1999, I wished I had taken him up on the offer, and years later when Robbie released his swing album, I laughed when in one of his songs he sings the line, 'Kevin Spacey would call on the phone but I'd be too busy!'

In the week that we returned from Glasgow, we went out for the evening to hip Camden nightclub Underworld. It was the first time that we had been there and I absolutely loved the atmosphere and the music they played. I was having a really great time when I spotted Zoë Ball in the corner, chatting with her co-host at the time, Jamie Theakston. I told Lorraine and then we went off to continue dancing. A while later, we noticed Jamie was standing at the edge of the dance floor watching us and then he came over and asked me how I was.

I told him that I was really happy, having had a great summer at the Glastonbury and V97 festivals and other events. We got talking and he asked if I wanted a drink and so we went down to the bar together and chatted while waiting to be served. We then took a table in the corner and Zoë came over to say hello. Jamie asked where we were going later and, as I was still friends with Bob, I had been planning to go to the Townhouse studios to hang out there for a while. I told him that they had a late bar and we could get something to eat, but he persuaded me to go to his flat instead. We set off in a taxi to his flat (not that far from Robbie's) in Notting Hill Gate with Lorraine and a couple of Jamie's friends too.

Inside his flat he had a huge music collection and together we chose some tunes to play while drinking a bottle of red wine. He had a games console set up with a driving game and we took turns, although I was so drunk by then that I don't think I did a very good job! On returning from the bathroom at some point, Jamie stopped me before we reached the others back in the lounge and started kissing me. We returned to the lounge and had a bit of a smoke and I was dying to tell Lorraine that I had kissed him! It wasn't long, however, before I had reached my limit and passed out on his bed!

The next morning I took Jamie's keys and went out to get us all breakfast. We then took a walk to Portobello market, where we ran into Richard E. Grant – it was like being in some sort of weird dream! In the afternoon Jamie went off to work and Lorraine and I went to the *TFI* studios in Hammersmith, although not for Take That this time, but purely as something to do and to take another friend who had not been before. Elton John and Kylie Minogue performed and then we headed back to Jamie's flat for the evening. My time with Jamie was fun – he is a really sweet and kind guy – but it wasn't long before he was dating Natalie Appleton from the All Saints so after that I didn't see him any more.

Liaisons with TV presenters aside, we were back on our mission to track down former members of the boy band Take That and next it was the turn of Gary. We had received a telephone call from chauffeur Jez, who told us that Gary was booked on a flight to Atlanta on 15 September and that he would be dropping him off at Gatwick airport. He gave me the time and the terminal, and told me that Gary was flying with Delta Air Lines.

Unfortunately, Lorraine couldn't make it that day due to work commitments and so I went along by myself, into new territory – the airport! After Jez had dropped Gary off, he called to let me know and I said that I was there. I made my way to the Delta Air Lines check-in desk, but there was no sign. On my way back down the escalator, I couldn't believe my eyes when I spotted Gary completely alone in the McDonald's, having some lunch!

I paced up and down the concourse by the shops, wondering what to do. Should I go and say hello, or was it rude to disturb a pop star while they were eating lunch? It would just be me and him and no managers, no other fans; I wouldn't find anything to say, I wouldn't be able to speak! All

I could picture was me going over to him, and then completely forgetting everything I ever wanted to say and looking like a complete and utter idiot, frozen like a statue, with Gary looking on, bemused. By the time I had paced around pretending to look at scarves and worldwide plug adaptors, I had built it all up in my mind so much that now there was no way that I could go over and say anything. I watched as he went up the escalator to the Delta check-in desk and I knew the moment was gone.

Less than two weeks after Gatwick, I went off to see Robbie in his first-ever UK solo concert in Woking. The venue was incredibly small, rather like a school assembly hall, but it was crammed full of the usual screaming, adoring fans. I had taken turns with some other girls to keep place in the queue all day to ensure that our front-row positions in this standing-only event were not compromised and now we stood excitedly at the bottom of the stage, waiting for Robbie.

It was the first time that I had heard 'Ego a Go Go' – which, before beginning, Robbie had told us he had written about Gary (ouch!) – and when he began to sing 'Back for Good', I just knew for a fact that this was not going to be any normal rendition! I frowned at Robbie (which he noticed), and then, when the chorus began and the song became all thrash, he looked back at me and smiled as if to say, 'Yeah, you were right, there was no way I was going to sing this Take-That style!' In the latter days of sell-out shows at Knebworth, how we missed the intimacy of those early gigs.

The venue that Robbie had been playing in was joined to a

hotel and I had booked a room there for the night. I got chatting to some of the staff there and they told me that after the show Robbie would be coming along one of the corridors to get out to his car, and so I waited at the end of the corridor by the stairs. After a while I heard Robbie's voice as he chatted with a woman (about cocaine of all things), and then when he was in front of me, I said, 'Excellent show, Rob, really good!'

With a towel around his neck, he thanked me very much, but I was frustrated because he must have heard that kind of thing all the time and I wanted him to know that I was being sincere. 'No, I really mean it,' I went on. 'It was really fucking excellent!' OK, maybe I shouldn't have sworn, but I had had a few bottles of beer and I really wanted to get my point across.

He looked up from where he had begun to descend the stairs and said, 'Thank you, thank you very much,' and then I watched from a nearby window as he got into his people carrier amid screams and flashes from some of the other hyped-up concert-goers.

7

GETTING TO KNOW GARY

The day after Robbie's Woking concert, I returned to London and met up with Lorraine near Liverpool Street station for the recording of Gary's 'Open Road' video, in which we were to be extras! Lorraine had entered and won a competition, and so there we were, all dressed up, hours before the scheduled start time, sitting on some steps opposite the square where this was all to take place and looking out for Gary. After an hour or so, he walked towards us, wearing a gorgeous brown leather jacket, on his way to his trailer parked a little way down the street, but, just as at the airport, I did not say anything to him.

As it began getting dark, lots of people started arriving, some of them professional extras and dancers, but most were competition winners. To avoid Interruptions to filming, Gary began the evening by spending a good twenty minutes chatting to fans, signing autographs and having photos taken before the recording was to start. I was wearing a sparkly blue sequin dress and blue jacket (they had advised bright and colourful) and waiting for my turn to speak to Gary. I had my photo taken with him and he asked me if I was going to be cold, but I told him that I would be fine because I would be doing lots of dancing. He said that he would too, and to illustrate gave us a little boogie.

After the impromptu meet-and-greet, extras (professional and fans) were positioned in a circle around some musicians and then Gary came into the middle of the circle ready to perform. The music began and it was our job to dance and clap while Gary and the assembled band performed 'Open Road' over and over again, trying different camera angles and shots. Gary was then given a chair to sit on while a make-up artist retouched his face and he amused the crowd by showing us his photo-shoot faces, which included the moody look and the cheesy smile!

I stood looking at him and I was really dying to tell him what Robbie had done to his song 'Back for Good' the previous night, but I held back. I did want Gary to notice us, though, and I was trying to think of something that we could do that would set us apart or get his attention. Just next to the circle that we were all in was a set of steps leading up to a building with some scaffolding wrapped around it. I told Lorraine that we should go up there and dance, where we would also have a much better view, and so off we went, climbing up to continue the party from our high vantage point. My plan worked: it wasn't long before Gary spotted us and he stopped

Chatting to fans while the make-up artist goes to work at the 'Open Road' video shoot.

in the middle of recording and held his hand up to his forehead, squinting at us and looking puzzled. We shouted down 'Woo ha' at him, and he cupped his hand to his ear for a repetition but was soon told off by the video director for interrupting the recording and had to carry on with what he had been doing. Every so often, he glanced up to where we were dancing and I was thrilled that Gary had finally noticed us, just as I had intended.

The evening was then temporarily halted by a huge McDonald's truck arriving to deliver burgers and fries to all of the extras, while Gary disappeared back down the street to his trailer. By now it was getting very late, not to mention very cold, and we were all being gathered around in the circle again to await Gary's return. As he did so, shielding himself from the chilled air in a red puffa jacket, he walked straight towards us and said, 'Oh, they've come down from the scaffolding then!' He then proceeded to rummage inside his coat pockets and asked, 'Would you like to know what I've got in my pocket?' A little worried about what was coming next, I was relieved when Gary pulled out two handfuls of chocolates and asked if we would like one!

'What are those two doing dancing on the scaffolding?' Gary ponders...

Soon it was back to the recording and, despite having to dance and clap to the same song over and over again, between takes Gary made it enjoyable by doing silly things like the *Men in Black* dance or making various funny comments. By the early hours of the morning, a lot of people had gone home and it was getting quieter and quieter. It was also absolutely freezing, but, despite Gary repeatedly asking whether I was cold or not yet, I refused to admit that I had been wrong earlier and kept on protesting that I was fine. We did, however, sneak off and seek warmth in a security van at one point, with the heating up full blast; while sitting there, we spotted Jez, who came over to see how we were.

It was now nearly 4 a.m. and it had been a rather unbelievable evening if you consider that the usual encounters with the band last only for short periods of time and we had been in Gary's company for hours. All good things come to an end, though, and it was soon becoming clear that he would be leaving. He walked towards us and I put my arms out to give him a big hug and finally admitted that I was 'bloody freezing'! As we broke apart, somehow we managed to keep holding hands and he rubbed my fingers with his as he reached forward to hug Lorraine. I think I nearly died and went to heaven and we certainly talked about that night for many days, if not weeks, after!

In the month that followed the 'Open Road' video shoot, Lorraine and I set about finding out which TV shows Gary was scheduled to appear on; we were now keener than ever to see him. We started by contacting his record company, who gave us the number of a company that dealt specifically with Gary's TV and radio appearances. The number that we called gave us his full TV and radio schedule for the promotion of 'Open Road'. We then had to put in plenty of legwork, calling numbers to get information and tickets for the relevant shows. In some cases full-on begging and pleading would do the trick and in others remarkable blagging skills were required to achieve the desired results.

On the subject of TV shows, it is worth noting at this point that sometimes the shows that you perceive as being 'live' are, in fact, pre-recorded and often live shows (such as *This Morning*) pre-record sections and then play them as if they are live. For example, an artist promoting their new single may come into the studio to do an interview and be scheduled to end the show with a performance of their song, but this can be recorded straight after the interview, leaving the artist free to leave and get on with their busy life. Sometimes a band is billed as being on a show but it turns out to be a report on the set of their new video, so these are things that you can check out before you head off down to the studios. On how to obtain tickets, watch the credits of the show and look out for the names of senior people such as the director or the producer and then attempt to make calls to them. Sound important, tell them you run the artist's website and you need a couple of tickets so that you can report on the show and help to promote it. Or try being honest and say that you are a fan, who is desperate to come in and be a part of the audience. After all, they do want people there, so try your luck and you will be surprised what you can get away with!

The first show Gary was to appear on to promote 'Open Road' was the *National Lottery Show* and once again we made the familiar trip to the BBC TV Centre in Wood Lane. We had quite good seats and Gary spotted us almost straight away and gave us a smile. When we left, there was a rather large crowd of girls waiting at the gates for Gary and we just knew that we wouldn't get a chance to talk to him properly and so we decided to walk off down the road back to the car. Just as we were waiting for the traffic lights to change so that we could cross the road, Gary's Range Rover with its blackened windows passed us and we decided that we should wait a while and then call Jez. Once we had arrived home, we called him and he told us that Gary had pointed us out to him and said that we were the girls from the video shoot. I found it hard to believe that Gary would have been pointing us out to anyone; we were nobodies, after all, just another couple of fans in an ocean of adoring faces, but I couldn't help getting excited, thinking it might be true!

A few days later I was to get my answer when we showed up at the Fountain studios in West London for the recording of the *Talking Telephone Numbers* game show. Once again, we had spoken to Jez, who had told us that he would be dropping Gary off there at 3.15 p.m., which saved us another long wait in the cold. Unusually, there was only one other girl there to see Gary – I think she had come from Germany. As the car drove around the corner and slowly moved towards us, I was incredibly nervous but Gary had put the window down and was eagerly waving at us. As he stepped out of the car and walked towards us, he said, 'Fucking hell, it's cold!' and, while I was taken aback by his strong use of language, I was also pleased that he felt more comfortable with us now and could be more himself. I did, however, jokingly make him apologise for swearing in front of the ladies!

As he signed an autograph for the other girl, he turned to us and said that he had seen us at the *Lottery Show* the other night and had waved, but that we had ignored him. I quickly reminded him that we were unable to see through dark glass, to which he responded, 'Yes, that can be a problem.'

I had, however, got my answer and it seemed that Jez had been honest about Gary pointing us out to him.

'Have you seen the video yet, then?' Gary quizzed us and asked what we thought.

I told him that it was good, but that I was disappointed that I was only in it for about two seconds – well, if I was being totally honest, my *legs* were only in it for two seconds! We then had our photos taken with him again and this time we asked the other fan if she would take a picture of me, Gary and Lorraine, and we returned the favour by taking a picture of the two of them. As Gary was about to leave to go inside the studios, I plucked up the courage to be a bit cheeky and asked if he could get us into his Heart FM concert the following week; I was pleasantly surprised when, without hesitation, he answered 'Yes' – full marks for bravery and what a result!

Lorraine and I went off to a local café for a hot chocolate to warm up and talked excitedly about the fact that Gary had just said that we could go to his concert. We had tried really hard to get tickets but it was invites for competition winners only. It was to be the first time that he had played live for fans since becoming a solo artist and we wanted so much to be inside to see it. We returned to the studio and managed to secure some good seats a few rows from the front, and, when Gary came out to sit at the piano ready to perform 'Open Road', he spotted us again and smiled a few times. It seemed so great that things were going so well with him – he now knew who we were and we were getting to know him. After the show we walked back to the car that we had parked a little way down the road and,

At the Fountain Studios for *Talking Telephone Numbers*.

as we drove past the studio, we decided to pull over and watch Gary leave. Now there were many more fans gathered by the exit, but, as Gary pulled away in the Mercedes, he saw us and waved from the non-blacked-out front windscreen!

Over the next few days, we spoke to Jez again and he reliably informed us that Gary had pre-recorded *The Jack Docherty Show* and the Radio One *Breakfast Show*, saving us two wasted journeys, and so all we had to do now was wait for the Heart FM concert. November 11th arrived and Lorraine and I excitedly made our way to the Air recording studios in Hampstead, where the concert was taking place later that evening. We managed to park up opposite the studios, which saved us from standing in the cold, and soon we saw Gary pull up and get out of his car and talk to a few fans gathered outside. We walked over to him and said hello, but he seemed to be in a bad mood and not his usual cheery self. I asked him if he had sorted out getting us in and he said that he didn't know yet, but he would let us know later. He walked off and my heart sank – I had obviously been way too pushy in asking him in the first place and had pissed him off. Let us know? How would he let us know? He hadn't got our phone number and it was unlikely that he would come out just to look for us. I felt embarrassed and stupid, and I was sure I would never see him again. Quite clearly, I had blown it!

We went off to get something to eat and returned a while later to watch all the excited fans queuing and then going into the concert. I really wanted to go home, but Lorraine said that we should stay and see what happened at the end. We waited and waited until finally Gary emerged from the studios in a much better mood, clearly having had a good drink or several at the aftershow party. He came over to us immediately and apologised profusely for not being able to get us in; he insisted that he had tried and that he felt bad because we had waited there all that time. We weren't sure whether or not to believe him, but, because he had taken the time to come and apologise, we didn't need to feel bad any more and the evening ended with another hug from Gary and a restored happiness in Lorraine and me.

Almost a month later and we were off again to the Battersea Power Station in London for the Concert of Hope. The show was organised in part by Gary himself and the line-up included Robbie (the first time the pair had been seen together publicly since Rob had left Take That), the All Saints, Boyzone and Peter Andre. In previous years the concert had been attended by Diana, Princess of Wales, to raise money for her charities; as she had died a few months earlier, this concert was to remember her devotion to the Concert of Hope and to raise money for her memorial fund.

We arrived at Battersea Power Station without tickets and so the first thing we had to do was go to the box office, where we were amazed to be lucky enough to get fourth-row tickets, courtesy of the promoters! There were a good couple of hours before the show was due to start and so we got ourselves a hot cup of tea to try to stay warm and then we decided to give Jez a call. When he answered, he said that he was at the venue and that he would drive around to the artists' entrance to pick us up. As you can imagine, there was quite a large group of girls positioned at the entrance, with the line-up for the show being mainly young male pop stars! It was quite a thrill, then, to get into Gary's Mercedes, again in full view of the other fans, all trying to stare inside to see what was going on.

We drove to a nearby street to chat with Jez about what he had been up to since we last saw him. He then told us that the aftershow party that evening was being held at a nearby restaurant called the Villa del Cesari. We had really struck gold meeting this guy – he was making our lives so much easier – and, having seen the death of Diana just a few months ago, we had vowed never to take part in car chases with the guys ever again so it was just as well that (where Gary was concerned, at least) we wouldn't have to. Jez then had to leave to pick up Gary's girlfriend Dawn from Euston station and we walked back to Battersea.

The concert was fantastic, especially from the fourth row! Robbie opened the show with a few tracks from his album *Life Thru A Lens* and dedicated his newly released song 'Angels' to Diana, before performing his brilliant rendition of 'Back for Good'. He was followed by boy band 911, the All Saints, Damage, Peter Andre and Boyzone and then, finally, what we had been waiting for – Gary! He came on to the stage to huge cheers and performed the Black Crowes' hit 'Hard to Handle'. It wasn't long before he saw Lorraine and me, and beamed us a huge smile; he was to look our way several more times as he belted out 'Hang On In There Baby' with Rosie Gaines and

'Harvest for the World' with Ronan Keating. The finale entailed all of the acts coming back out on to the stage to sing the Beatles' classic hit 'Let it Be', and halfway through, as presenter Denise van Outen thanked everyone for coming, Gary and Robbie delighted the crowds by hugging each other to almost deafening screams.

Lorraine and I soon sped off with another couple of friends that we had bumped into and arrived at the nearby aftershow-party location. Two security guys stood at the entrance next to a red rope, but, as it was a restaurant and seemed to be a rather intimate affair, I was not about to try to get into this one! First to arrive was Peter Andre, who was really friendly and commented on how cold we must be and offered to get us a cup of tea from inside! Next in were 911 and Damage, quickly followed by Gary, who dashed in so quickly that he didn't even spot us. We were wondering if Robbie would show up too, but neither he nor the All Saints made an appearance.

A couple of long hours later and Gary finally left the restaurant and was in the midst of saying goodbye to someone when he caught sight of us over the person's shoulder. He came over and gave us a hug and a kiss, and said that he had seen us at the concert; he seemed genuinely pleased to see us, and our friends were amazed at how friendly he was. It certainly made up for the way I had felt at the Air studios, where I had feared that I had really annoyed him, and, as Gary got into the car (that we had driven round in just a few hours earlier), I was really looking forward to seeing him again. He definitely had us hooked now!

Only a week had passed and we were on our way to see Mr Barlow once more, this time in Birmingham. It was almost Christmas and I had been up in the Midlands visiting family anyway and so it seemed rude not to attend the nearby Hallelujah concert in aid of the Duchess of York's charity Children in Crisis. On this occasion Jez would not be driving Gary and so we did not have our usual supply of information; nonetheless, where there's a will, there's a way, or so they say.

On arrival at the huge Birmingham National Indoor Arena, it became clear that there were several possible entrances that could be used as an artists' entrance, leaving us with no more than guesswork as to which one was correct. It was one of the coldest days I can remember and I was adamant that I would not be freezing my ass off for hours, only to find out later that I had missed Gary! I had a bright idea and telephoned the stage door. 'Hi there, I was wondering if you could help me. I am Gary Barlow's personal assistant and we are just on our way towards the arena now and I need you to confirm which entrance we are supposed to use.'

It worked like magic and the man on the other end of the telephone told me that it was the service entrance and asked where I was now. I said that 'we' were still on the motorway and would be arriving soon. I hung up and we couldn't stop laughing as we made our way round the building to wait for Gary.

Unfortunately, this time my hard work did not pay off as Gary had decided not to turn up for the soundcheck and arrived so late that he sped past us and went straight inside.

By the time we got to our seats, the concert had already begun and, as soon as Gary had performed a couple of his songs, we ran right the way around the building again and back to the service entrance, eager not to miss his departure.

Soon, his car approached and ground to a halt in front of us. He got out and gave us another hug and a kiss. We chatted for a moment and he told us that he would be back before going to sign autographs for a small group of fans waiting nearby. I overheard one of them complaining that she had paid £20 for his fan club but had not yet heard anything back. She insisted she wasn't worried about the money, just where the stuff was, and that she would be happy to pay £100. 'Don't give him ideas!' I joked, and then Gary returned to us and asked what we were doing in Birmingham. I explained that I was visiting family for Christmas and that we were making a detour. We talked about his upcoming tour in a few months' time and he told us that he was going to release 'My Commitment' next (although this never happened) and that he was about to listen to some mixes of it in the car on the way home. After that he wished us a Happy Christmas and gave us yet another hug and kiss before leaving.

8

LOTTERY WIN AND THE 'OPEN ROAD' TOUR

In January 1998 my life was to change forever when I won a rather substantial amount of money on the National Lottery after correctly choosing five main numbers and the bonus ball. It definitely was a happy New Year for me! Lorraine and I had only been planning to go to a couple of the concerts on Gary's tour in March, but suddenly we were now free to add a few more dates into the itinerary. We also felt excited by the idea that, if we should discover which hotel he was staying in, now we could easily afford it.

The whole thing was like a dream: suddenly, I could buy the camera that I had been eyeing up for the last few months in the shop window opposite my flat and many a trip was made to Lakeside Shopping Centre to stock up with new clothes and make-up. In the weeks prior to the tour, I paid for Lorraine and me to have a fantastic holiday in Gran Canaria so that we could top up our tans, and when the holiday ended

we couldn't wait to get home and pack for Gary's first solo tour. He had been so nice to us the last few times we had seen him that we anticipated staying in a hotel with him would be even better.

On 11 March, we set off to Nottingham, unbearably excited and with huge amounts of luggage containing all of the new clothes and shoes we had been busy buying squashed into the boot of the car. The venue for the first concert had the usual collection of fans standing around, waiting for Gary's arrival for a soundcheck. One of the girls was touching the

At the Camelot offices to collect my lottery winnings!

door of the tour bus and marvelling at how Gary had also touched that very door. It was slightly weird (not that we were in a place to judge, I guess), but Lorraine and I decided to go and get a drink and wait for the concert elsewhere, hoping that we would instead get a chance to see Gary later in the hotel. This wasn't a bad move, as, when we returned to the venue, the girls told us that Gary had gone straight inside with his tour manager, Chris Healey, and had not stopped to chat. Perhaps, it seemed, this less friendly Gary was born of pre-show nerves!

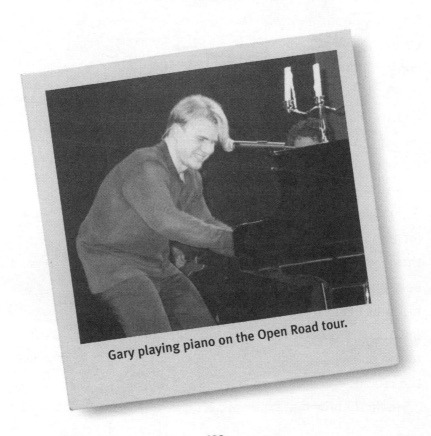

Gary playing piano on the Open Road tour.

Eventually, it was time for the doors to open, and in we went for the first of the eight concerts that we planned to go to on the tour. I was struck by how small the place was compared to the Take That shows; security was at a minimum and there wasn't much separation between us and the stage. We were in the third row and had a great view, and Gary saw us almost immediately after appearing on stage to open the show with Hue and Cry's hit 'Labour of Love'.

He looked to be a mixture of pleased and relieved that he had received such a warm reception from the crowd now it was just him up there on the stage alone. He sang some songs from his debut album and also a Take That medley that had everyone at their most lively! Once again he performed the song that he had recently sung at the Concert of Hope, 'Hard to Handle', and also Roachford's 'Cuddly Toy' with some very impressive (for Gary) sexy dance moves thrown in for good measure. When he returned to the stage for the encore, he came over to where Lorraine and I were, and posed briefly for us to take a picture. The show had been absolutely electric: Gary's voice always sounds so good live and he had even included a *When Harry Met Sally* moment after someone threw some chocolate on to the stage. He picked it up and said that he hadn't eaten chocolate in a very long time (hence his new slimmed-down look), but he proceeded to slowly unwrap the chocolate, take a bite and then lower his head on to the piano, moaning and groaning, to the absolute frenzy of the crowd.

His first show had been a resounding success and the next

thing we had to do was find his hotel. We were driving through Nottingham town centre, with me making phone calls to some of the hotels asking for his manager's name, when we spotted the tour bus at some traffic lights. We followed it to the Stakis hotel, where the band got out but there was no sign of Gary. We tried to book a room anyway, but they were full and so we had to sneak downstairs to the residents-only bar and hope that we could get away with sitting in there unquestioned. To order drinks from the bar, you had to show your room key, so we made sure that we brought a few drinks down with us from the public bar above.

It was very quiet in there and we were fairly nervous, thinking that Gary might walk in at any moment, especially when his band came in and took the table next to us. I recognised Paul Turner, Milton Macdonald and Mike Stevens, who had also played on the Take That tours. As my stepfather plays the bass guitar and had mentioned to me that he knew Paul Turner from a guitar shop in Birmingham, I used this to start a conversation with him. Paul knew who I was talking about, and asked how my stepfather and brother and sister were; soon Lorraine and I were chatting away to the band, which also included the drummer Chris Dagley and keyboard player Bernie Smith. They told us Gary was not staying at the hotel that night, as he had decided instead to drive home, but they did tell us the name of the hotel where they would be staying in a few days' time in Newcastle, which was lucky because we had never heard of it.

As it was Paul's birthday that night, the band were in the

mood to celebrate and happy to order us drinks using their room keys, although, when I told them that I had won the Lottery, they did expect me to buy a round! We talked about the Take That days and how it had all ended with Robbie and they continued to give us information about hotels and the itinerary for the rest of the tour. At one point, a suggestion was made that we should all go out to a nightclub, but in the end we agreed that we would go out in Newcastle instead. By about three o'clock in the morning, they decided that they should go to bed – there was another show the next night – but of course we did not have a bed! We said that we would probably drive on to Sheffield and then see them in Newcastle, and, as we hugged goodbye after a really great night, they said that we knew where they were if we couldn't find anywhere or if we needed them.

Not wanting to disturb our new friends, we headed off on a late-night trip to Sheffield and I booked us into the Stakis hotel there. We were really excited that we had got on so well with the band and that we now knew which hotels they were going to be staying in next. On arriving at the hotel, we ordered a club sandwich to keep us going while we booked into the hotels that had been disclosed to us that evening and we imagined how good the rest of the tour was going to be.

Later that morning, after a few hours' sleep and a filling hotel fry-up, we went off to the Meadowhall Shopping Centre to have our photos developed from the previous night's concert – all 150 of them! In the Take That days, cameras were not allowed into the arenas so this newfound photographic freedom had obviously gone to our heads. We were still a few years off digital cameras, so we ended up paying to develop a fair amount of really dodgy pictures too!

Soon it was show time again and we drove to the City Hall to see the second concert of the tour. Our seats were 19th row, so it wasn't until the lights went up for the 'Never Forget' arms-out, hand-clap bit that Gary finally saw us and gave us another winning smile. After the show we began the journey to Newcastle, having already been told by the band that they were doing the same. It became an incredibly long night when we somehow ended up going via Scarborough (check it out on a map – it's way off) and we arrived at the Malmaison hotel in the early hours, painfully tired and fed up. Once inside this unusual, but magnificent, hotel we soon perked up – it was absolutely stunning, very modern and almost gothic in design. We soon forgot all about the arduous journey that had brought us there and were sleeping soundly in the gorgeous Malmaison beds.

The next day we hung around the hotel, had some lunch and went out for a walk. There was no concert that night and so we were not sure if Gary would turn up or not, but we hoped he would. We saw the band in the evening and said hello, although they went to bed quite early, and, as it became clear that Gary was not arriving until the next day, we also had an early night.

The day of the third concert arrived and we were very excited about the fact that we had a concert and a high chance of an evening with Gary ahead of us. We decided to go shopping in the afternoon; we had come up with the idea to get some really saucy knickers to throw at Gary during the show as a joke, sort of Tom Jones style. We chose a red silky pair that had fluffy red feathers all along the top and we even sprayed them with a bit of perfume to complete the effect.

Outside the Newcastle City Hall, we could hear Gary rehearsing some songs during the soundcheck, including a new unreleased track called 'Superhero'. At the hotel in Nottingham, we had asked Paul Turner to tell Gary to add this to the set list and we wondered whether the advice had filtered through.

Once again we were in the third row, and so Gary saw us again and we exchanged smiles several times through another great performance. Despite being so close, there never seemed to be a good time to throw the knickers (I think I was a bit nervous of looking like an idiot) and so they stayed scrunched up in my hand, having not fulfilled their purpose... this time. Lorraine and I left the concert during the final song so that we could beat the rush and return to the hotel. We wanted to be sitting in the bar already when Gary walked in, so that it didn't look as if we had followed him. Once again, we became appallingly lost and by the time we got back to the hotel we were in a hurry to get parked and get a seat in the bar. The excitement that had been building inside now peaked when shortly after we had parked we saw Gary's Range Rover parked up too and knew that he must definitely be at the hotel.

Despite going up to our room to touch up hair and make-up after the concert, we made it into the bar, found a table and ordered drinks before Mr Barlow himself walked in and made his way to the bar. As he did so, he spotted us and his eyes opened wide. He walked straight over to our table. 'I've seen you every night so far,' he began.

'Yes, but we won't mention that because it's embarrassing,' I replied, forever worried what Gary would think of us. I told him that I liked his jumper, which had his initials GB on the front, and then we talked about how the tour was going so far and which bits we really loved.

We asked him why he wasn't doing 'Superhero' as we had heard him rehearsing it earlier in the day and he said that he would do it 'just for us' the following night. I told him that our seats were not very good at the next day's show but that we were front row in Birmingham, and so he said that he would do it there. I also told him that I had something funny to throw to him that night too and he said he would catch it. We then talked about what a gorgeous hotel the Malmaison was, and he said how the band hadn't liked the hotel in Nottingham. I told him that I knew that, as we had sat up drinking with them all night.

I then asked if Paul had told him that I had won the Lottery and, looking puzzled at me, he said that he hadn't. 'Yeah, I won the Lottery,' I said, remembering the past two months and how I had looked forward to telling him.

'Fuck off!' came his rather abrupt reply. 'You've won the Lottery?' he questioned.

'Not millions,' I explained. 'I had five numbers and the bonus ball.'

Gary seemed genuinely shocked and asked me what it had felt like to win, where I had gone to collect the cheque and what I had been spending the money on. He shook his head in amazement, and, as there was no spare chair, he was now crouched down next to us and resting his head on his folded arms on the table as he listened intently to my story.

'We're going to Dublin now,' I announced, feeling safe that I had given him a somewhat plausible explanation as to why I was suddenly spending my life following him on his tour.

'Dublin?' he asked, looking surprised, and then Lorraine asked him if we would be able to get tickets when we got there as it was a last-minute thing and we didn't have any. Without hesitation, Gary said we were not to worry and that he would get us into the two Dublin concerts and then he leaned in to Lorraine and said, 'We have to stay in with her now.' But I argued that he didn't have to stay in with me – he was far richer than I was. He advised me that, if I invested wisely and looked after it, the money could look after me for the rest of my life, to which I joked, 'Gary, have you not seen the way girls shop?'

We then got into a discussion about how we kept on getting lost as we were driving from city to city and Gary thought it both ridiculous and hilarious that we could have driven from Sheffield to Newcastle via Scarborough. Lorraine asked him directions to our next stop, Manchester, and he was happy to oblige. At this point his tour manager came over with a mobile phone and told Gary that he had a call. 'Is he there now?' Gary enquired, and then he stood up, promised to see us later and went to take the call. He went to sit round the corner with the band, leaving Lorraine and me to replay the conversation and order in a few more drinks, ecstatic that Gary had been so friendly and had agreed to get us into his Dublin shows.

A while later, Gary's parents entered the bar and he went to talk to them; all three left and we were gutted, thinking that he had gone to bed. The barmaid then came over to us and asked, 'Would you like a drink courtesy of Gary Barlow?'

While Lorraine and I had been anticipating a good night with Gary, this was exceeding all expectations! I think it was just the fact of being paranoid that Gary would think we were really stupid or annoying for following him around, but that this behaviour showed us that, in fact, he thought we were OK. We joked that these drinks were the best we had ever tasted, but were also confused as to why Gary had gone without saying goodnight.

Our question was answered when he returned to the bar and went to sit with the band again; he hadn't gone to bed at all. I called a waiter over and asked him to ask Gary if he would like another drink, as I wanted to return the favour. The waiter returned with a message from Gary to say thank you, but that he wasn't drinking any more that night. It wasn't long, however, before he was walking towards us and we thanked him for our drinks. 'You are very, *very* welcome,' he said, smiling, and then he sat down at the table next to us, which had become free, and he was joined by Paul Turner and drummer Chris Dagley and we said hello to them again. By now, I was really drunk, which helped me cope when Gary leaned backwards, practically leaning his head on my shoulder, to ask if I had a spare cigarette. Had I been sober, I would probably have gone bright red and passed out or something equally ridiculous! I gave him a Marlboro Light – Lorraine and I had brought hundreds of cheap ones back from holiday, which was handy since the nerves and excitement of the tour had us smoking about forty a day!

I suggested to Lorraine that, instead of sitting in the bar and waiting for Gary to leave, it would look much cooler if we went to bed, leaving him in the bar – it might perhaps help us to retain the teeny-weeny amount of dignity that you almost certainly lose doing this kind of thing! Hard as it was to do (especially since Gary was drunk and being friendly towards us), I put my hand on his back and told him we were going to bed, as we were really tired.

'You're not ducking out on me, are you?' he asked, while somehow taking hold of my hand and being very affectionate with it.

'Look at the state of you!' I said, noticing how drunk he actually was and how he was slightly slurring his words.

'I know,' he said, 'I don't normally drink when I have a show the next night either.'

I looked down to where he was still holding my hand and told him that he was being very naughty.

He then asked when he would see us next, and, although I was finding it hard to concentrate, I explained that we probably wouldn't see him in Manchester, but that we looked forward to front row in Birmingham. I then bent forward to give him a kiss goodnight, and after Lorraine had done the same we left the bar, seriously wondering if we had done the right thing in deciding to go. All the time we had spent trying to find him and then, when we did, we left! But, you see, there are so many people trying to get Gary's attention that I felt we needed to be that little bit different and so far it definitely seemed to be working!

After breakfast the next morning, we saw the band gathering in the reception area of the hotel, getting ready to leave and looking tired and hungover as we said good morning to each other. We returned to our room to pack, and, by the time we left the hotel, they had already all gone. On the motorway down to Manchester, we caught up with the tour bus and it looked as though Gary was sitting in the front, although it was hard to tell as the windows were mirrored. We drove on ahead to the Manchester Apollo and sat in the car, waiting for the tour bus to arrive. There was a good crowd at the stage entrance and, as Gary and the musicians hurriedly walked inside, there were loud screams and a multitude of camera flashes. We filled the next couple of hours by having some dinner at a nearby pub and managed to exchange our balcony tickets with a tout for some on the floor. Once inside, we wished we had not bothered as they were quite far back but it seemed as though the tout had not managed to sell our tickets and so we went up to the balcony anyway.

Once again we left the concert early but found that the car was blocked in at the small Apollo car park and so we couldn't actually go anywhere. As we stood waiting, we saw Gary emerge from the venue in his Range Rover, being driven by his dad – they were having great trouble driving away too. Someone was driving towards them on the incredibly narrow street, completely obstructing their speedy getaway, and soon the audience were leaving and starting to crowd around Gary's car. The car in front tried to reverse down the street so that Gary could get away (he was surrounded by girls tapping on the window and taking photos). Eventually, when the car was out of the way and the exit clear, Gary finally sped off to the screams of the girls that had been accompanying him along the road, with one girl shouting, 'I love you, Gary,' as he disappeared around the corner.

In the week that followed, we were back at home (Lorraine and I having moved into a gorgeous big flat together in London, courtesy of Camelot) and very much looking forward to the next concert in Birmingham and those extra-special front-row tickets. Gary had promised to perform 'Superhero' and 'just for us' and I had told him that I was going to throw something at him that he should catch. The only problem was that halfway up the motorway to Birmingham I realised the sexy red fluffy G-string was still at home! I decided that, if it was not meant to be with the sexy knickers, then I would do the exact opposite, and I don't think you can get quite as contrary a replacement as size 42–48 maternity knickers from Mothercare! Imagining me throwing them at Gary made us laugh until it hurt all the way to the till and right out of the shop.

At the venue, we met up with my mother (for whom I'd

secured a last-minute ticket) and I excitedly filled her in on all the gossip from the tour and showed her the pants I was planning to throw. She always thought I was mad with my big ideas to meet Take That but couldn't help but appreciate the success I was having at it! My father was rather more harsh, warning me not to waste all of my Lottery winnings 'chasing Gary Barlow all over the place' but I would always argue back that I was having the time of my life!

It was then show time and so we made our way to our front-row seats and marvelled at how we were practically going to be on stage with Gary, we were that close. Being in the front row was definitely in my Top Ten Things to Do Before You Die list – no one's big head to get in your way! When Gary came out on to the stage, he smiled and kept smiling at us throughout the first few songs. He wasn't just a pop star to me any more; this was someone who knew who I was, someone that I had been drinking with a few nights earlier and someone who now felt like a friend.

When Gary sang 'My Commitment', he encouraged the crowd to wave their arms in the air but couldn't help laughing at Lorraine and me, who had decided to do a small finger wave instead. When the lights went down on him and the spotlight shone on Mike Stevens for his solo saxophone performance, Gary even pointed out Mike's strange leg movements to us and then started doing an impersonation of them. Even up on the stage in front of thousands, he was conversing with us and of course that felt amazing.

The best bit was still to come, though, as, when Gary was

halfway through 'Cuddly Toy', instead of staying on the left-hand side of the stage (as we had seen him do at all the previous shows), he stood directly in front of Lorraine and me. We looked at each other and questioned whether he was doing it on purpose or if it was just a coincidence. He then began pulling the sexy dance moves (which included some vigorous pelvic thrusts) so close that I didn't know where to put my face and I'm quite sure I turned a bright shade of scarlet, especially with my mum looking on! Judging by the cheeky grin on his face, I became sure that he had done all this on purpose – what a tease!

Gary holding up my big pants!

Towards the end of the show, I knew that I had to throw those huge pants Gary's way and, catching his line of sight, I motioned with my eyes that I was about to throw something and he motioned back that he would catch it. He did, but he then held up the huge pants for everyone to see. 'Bloody hell! Whose are these?' he enquired. 'Have you just been wearing these, love?'

The whole thing was a bit of a blur to me so I asked Lorraine what had happened and she reassured me that it had gone down well and everyone had found it very funny – phew!

After the show, we ended up following Gary's tour bus, thinking it was headed to a Birmingham hotel – only it wasn't and soon we had followed it all the way on to the motorway. The next show was in London and we guessed that they must have been going straight there, which wouldn't necessarily have been a problem had my mother (who lived near Birmingham) not still been in the car! She kept asking if we could let her out but we wanted to follow the tour bus. When my stepfather called to find out where my mum was, she had to tell him that she had been kidnapped! We followed that tour bus all the way to the Hilton hotel in Kensington, London, and then had the awful realisation that we would have to drive all the way back to Birmingham to take my mum home – we must have been crazy!

Three days later, Gary's tour reached London with a sell-out performance at the Royal Albert Hall. We started drinking early as we began getting ready to go to the show, playing Gary's album full-blast from our flat and dancing so much at the window that passers-by stopped to look up at us. We were really happy, though – things couldn't have been going any better: Gary had made us feel so special and we couldn't wait to see him again. We took the tube through London, giggling as we did, and then enjoyed our sixth 'Open Road' tour concert, even though we were not quite so close to the stage this time!

There were quite a few celebrities at this concert, including Andi Peters, 911 and Boyzone, and in one of the boxes sat Gary's family and his girlfriend Dawn. After the concert ended, we bumped into Jez, but, as the drummer Chris was around, not to mention Gary's parents on their way to the aftershow party, we didn't speak.

Lorraine and I decided to go for a meal and we were walking down the road some twenty minutes later when we saw Gary's car parked up at the side of the road. The window started to lower, but it was only Jez, who was waiting to pick up Gary and take him home after the party. We chatted for a while and told him what had been happening so far on the tour and then we went off to the Hard Rock Café for a late-night meal before returning home.

The next day we realised that our next scheduled concert was Dublin and nothing had been formally arranged with Gary as to how we would get our tickets. The only show left between now and then with a hotel so that we could speak to him was Edinburgh. The band had told us they were staying at the Malmaison there too, but could we justify such a long journey? What would Gary think of us, driving hundreds of miles to see him? In the end, we decided we should just go, and it turned out to be one of the best nights with Gary that we ever had.

We set off from London early for the long drive up to Edinburgh. I had been too lazy to put on any make-up, deciding that, as we were not going to the concert, I could spend the evening in the hotel getting ready. We arrived at the Malmaison at about 4 p.m. The tour bus was parked outside and we saw Paul Turner walking towards it to get on. He gave us this look of surprise, not quite believing that we had come all the way up to Scotland. We smiled anyway – I must admit that I was feeling a tad embarrassed, but I needed to focus: we couldn't let Gary get away with another broken Heart FM-style promise, and we had to know things were OK before we flew out to Dublin!

After checking in, we spoke to Bernie in the reception area. He told us that after that night's show they were going straight on to Dublin. My heart sank: had I really just driven all the way to Edinburgh for nothing? Bernie told us that he didn't know which hotel they were going to be staying at in Dublin and I explained to him that Gary had promised us tickets, but nothing had been arranged.

Bernie said that Gary was doing a radio interview in the bar and through the glass I could see him chatting on his mobile. He offered to pass the message on to Gary after he had finished. Now I don't know about you, but when you meet your favourite pop star you probably want to look your best, right? Hours of prep work go into the face and clothes, hundreds of discarded outfit choices lie on the bed before you make your way out, looking super-gorgeous, to the hotel bar. Even if he's not single, you still want to look nice and there I was, no make-up, wearing a tracksuit and having just driven up from London after an early-morning start – I really couldn't have looked worse. I cursed myself for being so lazy – why had I not just put a bit of make-up on? But there was no time: Gary was about to come out and speak to us and I couldn't miss it so I had to grin and bear it. Not only did I not look good, I hadn't even had a drink yet and so I was *really* nervous!

Lorraine told me he was on his way out from the bar and my stomach flipped three hundred and sixty degrees. I looked up and there he was, with the usual wide-eyed look with which he often greeted us. I looked back and smiled, and then summoned up the courage to ask, 'Can we sort Dublin out?'

He replied, 'It's sorted,' and then he got the tour manager Chris to come over and write our names down on a piece of paper.

We were going to be on the guest list, *Gary Barlow*'s guest list – how exciting! Looking down at the vast amount of bags at my feet, Gary asked if I had been spending all my Lottery money and I told him that I was certainly having some fun.

Feeling a bit more relaxed, I stood up and planted a kiss on Gary's cheek, thanking him for Dublin. He then asked me if I would be staying after the show in Dublin. 'What do you mean?' I asked, puzzled. He explained that there was a strip show after his concert and I asked him if it was males or females. 'Female,' he responded and I just smiled, feeling a bit confused as to why he had brought it up.

As he went to walk away, I said, 'See you in Dublin then,' and he frowned at me and asked, 'Why? Are you not staying here tonight?' I told him that I was and he said, 'I'll see you later then,' and off he went.

I breathed a huge sigh of relief: the band were going to Dublin that night but Gary was staying in the hotel with us. Not only that, but we were now on his guest list for Dublin.

Up in the room (well, suite – I had splashed out this time), I looked at my face in the mirror. Could I have looked any worse? Probably not, but now Lorraine and I had a good few hours to have a big bubble bath, play some music, have a few drinks and try on lots of clothes before Gary was due back at the hotel. We ordered up a huge jug of orange juice from room service to go with the bottle of vodka I had brought with me and some little bottles of Coke to go with Lorraine's Southern Comfort. We played Nirvana's 'Smells Like Teen Spirit' at full volume and I remembered how I had felt seeing Gary perform it on the 'Nobody Else' tour three years earlier and I got really excited about the evening ahead in the bar.

By the time we were finished, the room looked as though some kind of bomb had hit it: clothes were strewn across every surface, ashtrays were full and yet more Marlboro Lights packets were piled high on the table next to the vodka and Southern Comfort. Finally, we were ready to go down to the bar and carry on the drinking there.

The bar area was empty as Gary and any other fans staying

ove left and right: The first time I met Jason and Mark, Copthorne Hotel,
tember 1994.

w left: A TV presenting triumph for Robbie at *The Big Breakfast*, August 1995.

right: Mark's 'Green Man' painting.

Above: Mark with fans at the Athenaeum Hotel, London, in February 1996.

Below left: Robbie at the Soccer Six event, May 1997.

Below right: Mark with Scottish fan Claudia in Southampton, August 1997.

Above: Mark at Uri Geller's house, August 1997.

Below: Lorraine, Gary, Me! *Talking Telephone Numbers* recording, November 1997.

Above left: Gary at the Morgan hotel in Dublin, March 1998.

Above right: At the Townhouse studios, London, in July 1998.

Below left: At the Sarm West recording studios, London, in February 1999.

Below right: By the river Thames for the *GMTV* broadcast, June 1999.

Above left: Gary with his most dedicated fans in Cornwall, December 1999.

*Above righ*t: Lucy with 'Paul' in Brighton, December 1999.

Below: Group photo of us with Gary's musicians, Bournemouth, December 1999.

Above left: Mark arriving for *This Morning*, 2000.

Above right: Gary performing in Hamburg, Germany, in October 2007.

Below left: Mark shows off his guitar playing skills at the Hamburg show.

Below right: Mark holding up a 'get well soon' banner for Howard, who was backstage recovering from a collapsed lung.

Above left: Jason performing at the Birmingham NEC, November 2007.

Above right: Gary poses with my sister Hayley at the Hotel du Vin in Birmingham.

Below left: Howard and his 'new fiancée' Amy at the Hotel du Vin.

Below right: Gorgeous Mark…

Above: Take That performing the outstanding 'Shine.'
Below: With Mark at the Hotel du Vin, Birmingham.

at the hotel were attending the concert and so we took a nice table by the front window and waited eagerly for his return. Slowly, the bar began to fill up with girls and I knocked back drinks at an alarming rate – at one point there were six empty glasses on the table, all belonging to me! When Gary returned to the hotel, he spent some time outside chatting to fans and signing autographs, and then we heard him go through reception and up to his room.

The bar was really busy now, with everyone waiting for Gary to come down. But it wasn't long before he graced us with his presence and what a buzz it must have been for him to see all those girls dressed up and crammed into the bar just waiting to see him! He had chosen a much more relaxed outfit of a tracksuit to mingle with his most dedicated fans. There were quite a few familiar faces in the bar, girls and women we had seen at the concerts and hotels along the way – it wasn't just Lorraine and me that were loopy enough to behave in this way!

Gary stood at the bar, chatting to another man and seemingly unaware that all eyes were on him. After some time, I went to the bar to get another drink. When I ordered my drinks, he turned to look and we said hello to each other and then began chatting about the tour and the shows that had taken place in between Newcastle and Dublin. Then he brought up Birmingham and the 'Cuddly Toy' incident. He admitted that he had done it on purpose and explained, 'I had one foot in front of Lorraine and one foot in front of you,' and then in the crowded bar in front of everyone he started reenacting the pelvic gyrations he had done on stage that night. I slapped his arm and I told him I didn't need reminding, thank you – it was not the sort of thing I would ever forget! Gary, meanwhile, was laughing his head off, thinking he was really bloody clever.

I then reminded him that he had said he would do 'Superhero' for us there, but he had failed to honour his promise.

'Couldn't be arsed!' he said, and I laughed at his sharp response.

I loved that he was being more normal with me rather than thinking he had to be so polite all the time. I requested my drinks be put on to room 43 and I asked Gary if he had heard my room number and he said, 'Yeah, I'll put my drinks on there later!'

I then went back to my seat and filled Lorraine in on the conversation. She had been pretty puzzled as to what was going on and being said and told me that plenty of people had been watching.

I looked up at Gary again and he was now alone at the bar. Despite everyone being there to see him, no one had the confidence to go up and speak to him. It was all a bit odd, but in my drunken state I decided to go back to the bar to talk to him again. He started talking to me straight away and this time he was being even ruder than before, explaining that, after the big pants I had thrown at him in Birmingham, he had had some even bigger ones thrown that evening. He leaned in to me to tell me that they had still been warm, then moved away, before turning back and leaning in to me again to give me the bonus information that they were also *yellow*. I slapped his arm again (playfully, of course) and told him that was a little too much information.

I explained to him that originally I had got a sexy red silk G-string with fluffy feathers all around the top to throw but, having forgotten them on the way to the concert, I had gone for the complete opposite instead and described to him how much fun it had been buying them from Mothercare. In the midst of this, he referred to us by our names, Lorraine and Claire, so I congratulated him on remembering. He thanked me, but remarked, 'Tomorrow you will be Richard and Judy!'

I then apologised to Gary about how abrupt I had been in the afternoon, asking about Dublin, but that I had thought he wasn't staying in the hotel that night. He said it was OK and then asked if I was going to be on the same flight as him. I told him that I didn't know his flight and so he told me that he was flying out to Belfast at 12 p.m. the next day because he had to do a TV show there first. He then said that he was leaving the hotel at quarter to ten the next morning. I found it so funny because this was the kind of information we always strived for and worked so hard to get and here was Gary himself dishing it out to me, but it wasn't to end there.

He told me there was a great nightclub in Dublin called the Pod and that he was going to be there one night. Confused at this outpouring of information, I asked Gary why he was telling me all this: since I was a fan, didn't he realise that I would now go there too? But he just looked at me and said, 'I know.'

I was finding it all a bit bizarre and so I changed the subject and told him that I was afraid of flying and was really worried about my Dublin flight. He started to ask which airline I was going with, referring to Aer Lingus as 'Air Flingus', and insisting that whichever airline he guessed that I was flying with was a dodgy one.

Despite the teasing, I offered to buy him another drink, but just as in Newcastle he politely refused. I insisted it wouldn't break the bank and we laughed. He gave in and asked for a Southern Comfort and lemonade but then again rather bizarrely announced that he knew what both Lorraine and I drank. I covered the contents of my glass with my hand, but he didn't even need to look. Instead he just continued, 'You drink vodka and orange and Lorraine drinks Southern Comfort and Coke.' I wasn't really quite sure what to say to that, but I suggested that maybe he had found out by looking at his Newcastle hotel bill, where he had kindly bought us drinks. He didn't respond, he just kept smiling and looking into my eyes. At this point I had no idea what was going on, but he seemed to be enjoying whatever it was that he was doing.

I told him that I was going to go and sit back down, conscious that I had left Lorraine on her own for some time and of course bursting to tell her everything that had just been said. She also couldn't believe he had given away such information and concluded that he must like us and that was a good thing, considering we were forever worrying about pissing him off or coming across as total loony tunes!

After a while, 'Love Won't Wait' came on in the hotel bar

and, once Gary realised, he laughed and then looked embarrassed. As I passed him on my way to the toilet, I put my arm around his shoulder and asked him if he was going to sing. He put his hand on my arm and laughed, 'No, I'm sick of the bloody song!'

By now the hotel and bar were much quieter as the non-residents had been asked to leave. When I returned from the toilet, I stood at the bar waiting to get served when two guys started to chat to me and offered to buy me a drink. Gary leaned back on his chair and knocked into me, but as I was drunk I thought I had bumped into him and so I said sorry. He then leaned back again but once again I said sorry! It was only afterwards that Lorraine explained to me that Gary had been doing it on purpose and laughing as I kept apologising. For a third time, he leaned back on his chair and elbowed me, but – as described by Lorraine later – was disappointed when I didn't respond.

Finally, I recognised that Gary was trying to get my attention and so I asked him what he wanted. He took my hand and said, 'I love your nails,' while gazing at my fingernails that I had painted a dark red. I crouched down by the side of his chair (I think it was that or fall down!) and replied, 'Oh, you like red nails, do you?' He turned towards me and smiled, and my heart banged hard inside of my chest as I wondered where this was going. I told Gary that I needed to sit down; I had meant back at my own table, but Gary told me to sit on the empty chair next to him. I asked him if the person who had been sitting there before me would mind, but he told me it was OK.

Lorraine walked over and handed me our room key, explaining that she was going to the toilet, and Gary commented that she looked stressed. He asked if we had been friends long and I explained how we met and how lovely Lorraine was. He was then curious to know how much time we had taken off work to come and see him. I said that I wasn't working, following my Lottery win, but that Lorraine had booked quite a few days off. As we chatted, I felt more relaxed and suddenly a flood of things entered my head that I had wanted to say to Gary, but up until now had not been able to.

He had recently released a video called 'Open Book', which followed him around the world as he promoted his first album. In one section he is lying on a hotel bed in Kuala Lumpur with a Malaysian assistant called Karen by his side, and he is trying to embarrass her by pretending he is on the phone to someone and describing how he has four girlfriends. Not only that, but how he has sex with all four of these girlfriends every night. The shocked assistant's jaw drops and then Gary hangs up the phone and does a really dirty laugh. Once Karen realises that she has been the victim of his wicked sense of humour, she throws a big cushion at him and shakes her head.

I told Gary this was my favourite part of the video and I asked him if he would do his dirty laugh for me, but he said that he simply couldn't do it to order! Instead, he began telling me about his time in Malaysia and what the women are like there but this time I thought it was my turn to wind him up and so I jokingly interrupted him every time he tried to speak until we were both laughing and I was feeling much more confident. I did take a moment to explain to him that I felt very stupid for following him around, but he just shook his head as if to reassure me.

When Lorraine returned from the toilet, she crouched down with her back against the bar and joined in on the conversation. We began discussing his band and, in particular, Gary mentioned how serious Bernie was. I told him that I had asked Bernie which hotel they were staying at in Dublin, but that he had told me he didn't know. Gary turned to ask tour manager Chris the name of the hotel and then told me it was going to be the Morgan. A while later I realised that I had forgotten this important piece of information and so I asked Gary to repeat it; this time he told Lorraine as he had probably recognized that she was not as drunk as I was. I muttered that we probably wouldn't get a room now as it would be fully booked, but Gary said, 'Yes, but we can only hope.'

He then turned his attention to my hair and pulled on a beaded braid that I had had done in Gran Canaria before the tour began. At the time, my hair was also half-blonde and half-brown (yes, on purpose!) and I explained to Gary that I got bored easily and liked to be a bit different. 'You're gonna end up like Dougie,' he laughed (Dougie being a nickname for the dreadlocked Howard Donald). I insisted I wouldn't, but Gary repeated just as fiercely that I would. The teasing wasn't to end there, though, as he once more turned his attention to my abject fear of flying, sharing his air-travel advice: 'Make sure you sit at the back of the plane as they don't reverse into the sea!'

This time it was Lorraine's turn to give him a slap. 'You're not the one that has to get her on the bloody plane!' she jokingly fumed.

After about half an hour of chatting with Gary, I was beginning to contemplate my position. As far as I was concerned, this just didn't happen: this was Gary Barlow, for Christ's sake, you don't just end up drinking with him into the night, not if you're a fan anyway! My insides were a heady mixture of not wanting this moment to end and worrying over where it was going. It really hit me that I was sitting with Gary Barlow – I felt that I had to really appreciate where I was, given that so much of my time and energy had gone into reaching this point.

At the same time, I was seeing Gary more as just a guy rather than a star and my deep thinking became words when I said, 'You're Gary Barlow, aren't you? Pop star.'

I think he understood what I meant; he lowered his head and replied, 'Supposed to be, yeah.'

Continuing in my deep (albeit drunken) thoughts, I stared at some coloured glass bottles on a shelf on the wall behind the bar and thought how amazing this year had been for me so far and how lucky I had been, and that evening was certainly no exception. 'I've never been this happy,' I announced, but then made a joke by adding, 'Well, not since last night anyway!'

We began to talk again about my Lottery win and Gary, being quite an expert, was forthcoming with financial advice, discussing investments and property. He told me about his homes in Cheshire and London and how his mansion

Delamere Manor had tripled in value after his extensive renovation work on it.

Following the rather more serious conversation, it didn't take him very long to lighten it up again by purposefully swearing as much as he could just because I had light-heartedly told him off for it. He chatted to Lorraine, adding in obscenities wherever he could, and all the while keeping one eye on my reaction and grinning once more from ear to ear – the man just loves to wind people up. Not satisfied with the incessant profanities, he then turned back towards me and let out an almighty burp.

'Oh, that's right, just burp in my face then!' I exclaimed.

'I just did!' he replied proudly.

I told him that he was 'So Northern' and we began a battle of North versus South, despite the fact that I myself am a Northerner and proud of it. I have lost my Geordie accent, having lived in the Midlands and then London for so long.

Gary started by saying that Southerners couldn't swear properly anyway, saying things like 'fak' instead of 'fuck', and progressed into everyday speech by attacking words that contain an 'a' that Northerners pronounce like the 'a' in 'cat' and Southerners treat like the 'a' in 'car'. When he said the word 'dancing', it made me think of his girlfriend Dawn, who is a dancer, and I told him, though Lord knows why – I blame the alcohol – that I had seen her at the Royal Albert Hall in London. I also then stupidly told him that we had seen Jez too, before quickly realising that we were not supposed to know Jez! I covered by saying that we had met him briefly during the 'Open Road' video shoot; he didn't seem to notice anything strange.

At one point, someone nearby asked what the time was and I said that I never wear a watch because in the past I always seemed to break them or lose them. Gary showed me his arms in agreement – he did not wear one either, only his Cartier 'Love' bracelet. We moved on to talk about music and I asked him if he liked Chante Moore, as I had always imagined that he would when I listened to her. He said that he did, and then mentioned one of his favourite singers, Eric Benét, and told us a funny story about the time he went to buy his album from the shop. He admitted that he had asked the shop assistant for the album by Eric *Benét* but pronounced it Eric *Bennet* and had felt quite embarrassed when corrected!

The pair of us even had a little thing going on as we chatted into the early hours of the morning that, if one of us started to ramble on a bit, the other would purposefully slip their arm off the edge of the chair to show boredom. Every time we did that, we found it so funny, really laughing in ways that I could not have imagined just a few hours before as I had been getting ready in the suite upstairs, hoping to be lucky enough just to say a few words to him.

Gary asked me if I had seen him on the *National Lottery Show* a few nights earlier and I told him that indeed I had. 'I was thinking about you while I was there,' he said softly. I felt touched for a moment before he continued, 'Yeah, I was thinking that bitch better not win again!' That is Gary all over – he loves to wind you up and gets a massive kick out of it, that's clear. You could almost see the cogs turning in his head as he thought up the next thing he could say or do to get a reaction. What always strikes me about him too is how different he is from the Gary you see on TV. He's been accused of being boring, almost monotone, in some interviews, but behind the scenes he's always joking and making everyone laugh. His jokes are filthy – sort of Bernard Manning cum Roy Chubby Brown – and no subject is out of bounds, but he knows how to make the people around him happy, especially two very lucky fans that night!

We went on to talk about clothes and how he loves to wear Versace because they make clothes for short people! He moaned about his height (or lack thereof) and how he wished he could grow a few inches (girly giggles all round) and Lorraine said that she wished that she was shorter, but Gary disagreed and said that in the past he'd always liked tall girls.

I took out a cigarette and offered one to Gary; he refused and said that he only smoked Silk Cut now. I said that I thought he smoked Marlboro Lights and that that was the only reason I smoked them. I was, of course, joking but was met by an odd look before I let on. I lit my cigarette and after a few moments became conscious that Gary had placed a Silk Cut between his lips and was staring at me as I had left him out when lighting my own cigarette. I apologised and lit it for him, and he then brought up the subject of strippers again, referring to the upcoming Dublin shows. Despite the repeated reference, he admitted, 'Girls gyrating in G-strings does nothing for me!'

I told him male strippers did nothing for me either as I preferred a more toned, but natural, body. For some reason this reminded me of seeing Jason Orange in the summer and the things he had said about his skinny legs. I told Gary how we had been at his old house not so long ago and had met Jason there, then shared with him the strange comment Jason had made about me going to get Gary's autograph instead of his because it would be worth more. Gary just shook his head in disappointment.

A man that had been chatting up Lorraine earlier in the evening came over and tried to engage in conversation with her once more (like you have a chance while she's talking to Gary Barlow!) and didn't seem to take the hint that she was not interested. To get him to back off, I told him that I was Lorraine's girlfriend and therefore she would definitely not be up for it. Gary's face was a picture and the man also got the message and left.

By now, it was really late but Gary didn't want to go to his room just yet, saying that he was sick of hotel rooms and wanted to spend as little time in his as possible. All in all, we were probably chatting there for about two hours, although as I had been so drunk it seemed to have passed more quickly. When Gary finally decided to call it a night, he leaned forward, took my face in his hand and gave me a kiss before kissing Lorraine and then going off to bed. Had any of that evening really happened? I was buzzing as we returned to the suite but soon passed out on the bed, sleeping it all off.

When I opened my eyes the next morning, I immediately

recalled the previous night's events and Lorraine and I went over what had been said. Despite Gary telling us what time he was leaving the hotel that morning, we gave it a miss and instead had some Scottish breakfast brought up to the room to settle our stomachs. If Edinburgh had been so great, what on earth was going to happen in Dublin? If I had thought of myself as being somehow hooked on the adrenalin, on the feelings that surrounded being with the band and now more especially Gary, then last night had turned me into some kind of horrible junkie, shooting up in the corner – it was hopeless! Excited by the prospect of my next 'fix', I made my way back down to London, consumed with everything that had been said the night before and everything that was still to come. There wasn't much time to recuperate before we were off to the airport to face the flight to Ireland for the final leg of Gary's UK tour.

I survived the dreaded flight, which was short and relatively free of turbulence (despite Gary's repeated warnings about crossing the Irish Sea) and soon we were in a taxi heading towards the centre of Dublin. As I had gloomily predicted two nights earlier, the Morgan hotel was fully booked, although only on the first night, and so we had to stay in a nearby bed and breakfast.

We asked the taxi driver where the Pod nightclub was and he explained, although he warned us that it was notoriously hard to get into and usually you had to be on the guest list. We dropped off our things at the B&B and quickly got ready before taking another taxi over to the Morgan to try to see

Gary as he arrived there. When we checked the place out, we were disappointed to see that renovation works were going on and, as such, there was no hotel bar. We were advised that we could drink in the Sports Café next door – but would Gary drink in there?

Once again we asked if any rooms had become available for that night but still nothing. As we stood in reception, Gary arrived at the hotel and entered the reception area. 'Oh no, don't let them in here!' he jokingly advised the receptionists upon seeing us.

We greeted him with a kiss and a hug, and then he and his party (which included his brother Ian and sister-in-law Lisa) checked into the hotel. I called Gary over and told him that we probably wouldn't be able to get into the Pod as it was a bit exclusive and we needed to get on the guest list. He said that he probably wasn't going to go any more so it didn't matter and then he said for us to enjoy the concert and that he would see us later.

He went off to his room and we went to the Sports Café for some lunch and a few drinks. Drummer Chris Dagley came in and joined us at our table for lunch. There were another couple of German girls who seemed to always be around and Chris told us they ran Gary's website. This actually turned out to be a fan site called GBNI or Gary Barlow News International, which provided a wealth of information about Gary during his solo years.

Later that afternoon, everyone gathered in the lobby of the hotel, waiting to go to the concert – even Ronan Keating from

Boyzone was there as he was to perform a duet with Gary that night. Gary's brother and sister-in-law spoke to me as they recognised me as 'the girl that won the Lottery' – Gary must have told them who I was earlier in the day after they had arrived. Then, for the seventh time that month, it was show time and we set off for the Olympia Theatre in Dublin.

On arrival, we went to the box office and said that we were on the guest list, but then had a mild panic when they couldn't find our names. Eventually, though, we were given our tickets and we were absolutely thrilled to find out that we had our own private box right at the front of the theatre and what a buzz to know we were guests of the star performer! Despite already having seen the show six times, both of us really enjoyed it and Gary managed to throw a few smiles our way during some of the songs. Although Gary had said earlier in the day that he might well not be going to the Pod after all, we decided to go there anyway just in case.

As you would expect on the door of such an exclusive nightclub, there were some heavy-duty bouncers and I knew I would have to use my best-ever blagging skills to get in. I told them we were on Gary Barlow's guest list and, despite this not being the case, I managed to sweet-talk our way into the club with a little charm. Unfortunately, we were so tired from driving back from Edinburgh and then flying straight on to Dublin that we couldn't keep our eyes open. After one drink I actually fell asleep on a swish sofa in there and, since there was no sign of Gary, we left soon after.

After a hearty Irish breakfast the next morning, we transferred to the Morgan hotel. Our room looked over the front entrance and we saw Gary go out on foot at lunchtime with tour manager Chris. We got ready for the eighth and final show of our personal adventure on the 'Open Road' tour, while feeling increasingly downhearted that Ireland was not turning out to be anywhere near as good as Edinburgh. Who knew when we would have another opportunity to see Gary like this again? Such high hopes had been dashed, largely because the hotel did not have a bar! It is tour protocol for band, crew and fans to meet in the hotel bar after a show, so, without this common meeting place, we really didn't have a chance to see Gary again as we had hoped.

Once again, we loved the show and tried to hang on to every moment since it was to be our last. That night our private box was situated on the opposite side of the theatre and was next to the one occupied by the guitarist's wife, who also asked me if I was the girl who won the Lottery. She said she had recognised me because of my hair (which was, as previously described, pretty unusual), and I was really getting the feeling now that I must have been discussed with those in the inner, *inner* circle, though I suppose that a Lottery win of that magnitude is pretty unusual.

As the show was about to end, we made a dash for the exit and sped back to the Morgan. We arrived there at the same time as Gary and thanked him again for the tickets and said that we had had a really great time. He told us that we were welcome, while shovelling lots of red liquorice into his mouth, and then went off up in the lift to his room to get changed. For a while we waited in the reception area and Gary soon came back down and posed for some pictures with other fans before Chris began rushing him out to his car outside. I had wanted a photo but settled for a hug and a kiss, and then he was gone.

We didn't know if he was going to the Pod, but I sort of gave up inside and was too tired to lie my way into the club again. Exhausted, we went up to our room to sleep. A few hours later, we heard a commotion outside and looked out. Gary was coming in, seemingly drunk again, and paused to talk to a few girls who had waited patiently for him by the hotel door. This is what we extra-dedicated fans do – a concert or an autograph is just not enough. It starts off quite small and grows to a full-on career of locating and spending time with your idol. Success does not cure the desire, but merely increases it, and the more you have, the more you want.

Along the way, I have met so many girls who have sacrificed their time, their money, their jobs – whatever it takes to spend a few moments with Take That. I only wonder if the guys ever really knew when they posed for a picture or signed their name the lengths those people had gone to and the hours they had waited for that precious moment. The next morning we had to leave so early for our return flight to Stansted that we didn't get to see Gary and so we just had to wait with uncertainty for our next opportunity to meet up with him.

9
SUMMER '98

After the excitement of the tour, we watched and waited for the release of Gary's next single, his next TV show or public appearance, but nothing came. Almost two months later, on 17 May 1998, we went to the Mile End stadium to watch Mark and Robbie play football, once again in the Soccer Six tournament. Wearing green football shirts emblazoned with the Challenge TV logo, Robbie and Mark showed off their footie skills to the assembled crowd of girls, who relentlessly screamed and shouted the names of their idols. As was tradition, it seemed, a blonde streaker wearing a black thong ran across the pitch close to Robbie but he just ignored her and carried on with the game.

One marked difference between this and the previous year's tournament was that Robbie was now enjoying huge chart success following the release of 'Angels' and was not seen wandering around drinking pints of beer! In fact, he was just about to kick off his second solo tour around the UK, and, on 1 June, I headed down to Brighton to see him play at the Event nightclub there. Now I find it unbelievable that Robbie ever played in a small tacky nightclub just off Brighton's shingled seafront – every time I drive past there, I laugh to myself.

Lorraine and I arrived at the venue in the afternoon and we were sitting opposite in the car when we saw Robbie leave from a side door with a male companion and walk off towards the beach. We quickly found somewhere to park and followed at a distance. But we soon located Robbie playing on some fruit machines in an amusement arcade under the Kings Road Arches. He wasn't wearing a disguise but he was not disturbed by anyone. I guessed that he would most likely be headed to the pier (that's what you do when you're in Brighton), and so we walked off ahead to dispel any notion he might have that he was being followed.

My guess proved right, and soon he and his companion were close behind en route for Brighton's famous seafront attraction. Though Robbie never noticed us, we kept a sneaky eye on him as he enjoyed some of the funfair-style attractions, trying to knock five cans over to win an oversized cuddly toy!

We went up ahead to the bar at the end of the pier – I imagined this was where Robbie and his pal would head to next and that it would look better if we were already in there. The plan backfired, and after about twenty minutes we realised that Robbie was not coming. We decided to walk back to the Event and on the way we saw Robbie again, but this time he was walking alongside none other than Jamie

Theakston! They turned a corner out of sight and I discussed with Lorraine what we should do. It had been quite some months, but surely if we went up to speak to Jamie then we would end up chatting to Robbie too?

After trying to weigh up the awkwardness factor of seeing Jamie again against the prospect of having a drink with Robbie, somehow I mustered up all the confidence I could find (without the alcohol that I usually relied on) and we continued walking. We saw Jamie just inside the Fortune of War bar and I took a deep breath and entered. He didn't see me at first and so I just stood at the bar, but then as he and his friends were about to make their way to a table by the window, I said Jamie's name and he walked towards me. 'Hi, long time, how are you?' I began. Surprised to see me, but nonetheless still warm and friendly, Jamie and I chatted for a while and he said that he was going to see Robbie's concert at the Event later. I told him that I was too and so he said that he would see me later. He went to join his friends at the table but Robbie was nowhere to be seen – he must have gone on ahead. A few hours later, we were inside the club being entertained by Robbie, who was performing tracks from *Life Thru A Lens*, including 'Ego a Go Go', 'Let Me Entertain You' and of course 'Angels'. It was a fantastic show, as always, but I didn't see Jamie again and we just decided to go home.

Three days later, I happened on an article in the *Daily Mirror* that said that Gary had split from his girlfriend Dawn. The story sounded ridiculous, with an allegation that Dawn had gone running straight to Robbie's house in London, and so I called

Jez to see if he knew anything. He said he didn't, but that he would be driving Gary later that day and dropping him off at the Capital FM studios at 6.30 p.m. Lorraine and I decided to go along – we were definitely keen for a reunion with Gary after what felt like a long time. Standing on a street corner waiting for a black Mercedes to arrive doesn't quite have the ambience of a bar in a luxury hotel, but we had to settle for it if we wanted to see Gary again. Even so, I couldn't have been less prepared for how different it would all seem compared to the late-night drinking session back in Edinburgh.

When Gary arrived, he put his window down and stuck his tongue out at the other two girls who were also waiting for him. He then drove past and pulled up further along the entrance to the studio parking area. When he got out of the car, he turned and waved, but then went inside. He probably was upset about what the tabloids had written that day, but it felt so cold, considering how we had been just a few months earlier.

For a while, we waited around and then Gary came out of the building and approached me. We hugged for quite some time and he asked if I had been missing him, to which I jokingly responded, 'No,' before adding, 'Of course I have.' I told him that I had bought the Eric Benét album and that I really loved it, and he seemed pleased. We talked about his upcoming plans, if he was going to America (as had been reported) and how his second album was coming along. He then went to talk to the other girls and I could hear them discussing the Internet and how Gary had been trying to get on to a particular website but had been struggling with it. Jez reversed the Mercedes out on to the street and I gave him a sneaky smile and mouthed 'thank you' at him and then Gary turned and got inside. He waved goodbye as he was driven away.

A few weeks later, it was back down to Brighton again for the Party in the Park. Gary would be performing a few songs there and we even found out that the band were going to be staying at the Brighton Metropole hotel the night before. We booked a room and excitedly checked in with high expectations of another great night with Gary Barlow – this time the hotel *did* have a bar!

As the evening wore on, we grew concerned that none of the band members scheduled to be staying there had turned up and there was no sign of Gary either. Growing more and more frustrated, I called reception and asked if 'my friends' had arrived yet and was mortified to learn that all of the reservations had been cancelled at the last minute! I suppose that's the risk you take when you go Take That spotting – there's really no guarantee that you will see them – but, in a sense, it makes it all the more exciting when you do have success. If anyone could have afforded a £250 mistake like that, it was me, but then there are some others who – like me in the beginning – got into a lot of debt just to see those guys! Hey, lads, what's this madness that you inflicted on us?

The next day, we went to Preston Park to wait for Gary, who had decided just to drive to Brighton on the day rather than stay in the hotel the night before. The park was busy, as was the artists' entrance, so, as I knew Brighton fairly well, I suggested we go and walk up the road towards the A23 as that was the way that Gary would be driving in. The traffic was moving very slowly and so hopefully we would get a chance to see him as he crawled down the road.

As predicted, the black Mercedes drove slowly along the London Road, its famous passenger protected by blacked-out windows, but experts such as us knew exactly who was inside. As we got nearer, Gary must have seen us and he put down the window just a little and started sticking his two fingers up and laughing. Some other people who had now seen him rushed to the car window and passed pens and pieces of paper through for him to sign. I felt slightly guilty that we had blown his cover, though I'm sure he didn't mind signing a few autographs. We walked alongside the car until it reached the park and Gary went off to prepare for the few songs he was to sing before making the journey back to London.

A week later, it was the big Party in the Park for the Prince's Trust that had us travelling to London's Hyde Park to see Gary again, although being among a crowd of 80,000 was even less intimate than the last few times we had seen him! With this in mind, we decided to leave the concert after Gary had performed his set to try to find the offices of his management company, Globe Artists. We had recently read in a magazine article about their existence and that they were based in Battersea Square. Ever willing to do a bit of detective work, we parked up in SW11 and had a wander until we came to a small, secluded square of shops and offices called Cotswold Mews. We walked inside and then there, right in front of us, was a glass door with a Globe sticker on the front and, to clarify that we had, in fact, found Gary's offices, there were gorgeous black and white framed pictures of the man himself inside.

Feeling happy that this could be a good place to see Gary away from the usual events that attract many other girls, we went to a café opposite the Mews to have a drink. Despite having known Gary's home address in London (a gorgeous flat overlooking the Thames, also in Battersea) for some time, I refused to take things to that level, fearing Gary would think I had gone way too far. However, for some reason these offices seemed acceptable, as they were, after all, connected to work and so we kept watch for any sign of him from the window of the café.

Remarkably, it had only been half an hour since our new discovery (and bearing in mind that it was a Sunday, too), but there was Gary in his VW, driving around the corner to pull into the Mews. We had to explain quickly to the lady in the café that we would be back to pay and we began to run across the square. There he was, carrying a box, with Howard Donald at his side walking towards the office! Excitedly, I carried on until I saw Gary's girlfriend Dawn was also walking with them and then I stopped in my tracks. I don't know why, but I didn't want to go and speak to him – perhaps I realised that this was his personal time that I was now invading and seeing him with Dawn reinforced that. We returned to the café and saw them all leaving shortly afterwards, but they never knew we were there.

A few weeks after that, I received a telephone call from Bob – he had been working the night shift at the Townhouse studios and had noticed that Gary was booked in for a few days the following week. This was great news! Gary would be recording at studios that I had access to. I had spent so many evenings at Townhouse with Bob and we pretty much had the place to ourselves through the night. We would make food in the kitchen, watch TV and enjoy free drinks. There was even a pool table upstairs that we could use and later ping-pong too. When Elton John recorded there, Bob showed me the studio he was using and the piano that he had had specially brought in to record with, which I sat down and played.

The night before Gary was due to arrive at Townhouse I went there to meet Bob. I even slept on the sofa in the studio Gary was to be using the next day! When morning came and the regular employees were due to arrive, I had to leave and so I walked to the tube station with Bob. As I was walking back along the road from the studios, I turned the corner and there was Gary, right in front of me, having just arrived. Startled and surprised by the timing of it all, I proceeded to come out with the most ridiculous thing I have ever done or said in my life (and there have been a few): I pretended I hadn't known Gary was going to be there!

I can't explain, and I don't know what took over me but I asked Gary what he was doing there and told him that I had stayed at a friend's last night and was just on the way to catch the tube home. Gary humoured me; perhaps it looked slightly plausible for a moment, but what a coincidence that really would have been, had I been telling the truth! We chatted as we normally did and he told me that he was there to record a few songs, but that he 'wasn't ready in himself' to bring anything out yet. I warned him that he didn't want people forgetting who he was – after all, Robbie's solo career was exceeding everybody's expectations and it had started to feel as though Gary was fading away.

Gary told me that he would be at the studios for three nights in total and I said that I would come back one day with Lorraine. He said that he was on the Internet (I thought he just meant that he used the Internet at home, but more on that later) and I told him that I was trying to set up a website on him but was learning it all from scratch so it was quite difficult. I also told him that I liked to write and would perhaps like to cover his next tour, travelling with him to Europe and beyond, while writing a book. He said that that was OK, 'as long as it is good', and I just smiled and pointed to myself as if to say, 'Consider the author!' I mean I was hardly going to write negative things about him, was I?

I remember him leaning back against the metal fence of the parking area as we chatted, and it dawned on me that, since I had said I didn't know that he was going to be there, I couldn't very well show up later for the night shift with Bob as he would realise! We said goodbye and I walked off, considering myself the world's biggest idiot and cursing myself for saying such stupid things. Gary must have known I was fibbing, but well done to him anyway for still being so lovely to me!

As suggested, two days later I returned with Lorraine and we waited outside until Gary drove himself to the studios and pulled up at the gates to the car park. We were amused that he had to go and get the key to unlock it and I asked, 'Aren't you supposed to have someone do that for you? You are supposed to be a big pop star!' He laughed and agreed (jokingly) that he should indeed, and then we posed for some pictures together. Whenever I had felt bad about seeing Gary or at any time felt awkward, he would always make up for it with big smiles and huge hugs that just made me feel so welcome – even in the photo taken that day he has both arms around me – and this would always leave me wanting more and thinking of when I could see him again.

Howard performing at Prague V.

With Howard's dad.

The summer was rounded off nicely with a trip up to Manchester to see Howard perform a musical showcase at Prague V on Canal Street as part of the 'In the City' music conference. Howard was still looking for a record deal to release his solo material and the venue was full of record-company types, a few lucky fans who had managed to get in and Adam Rickitt, who, like Howard, was managed by Nigel Martin-Smith.

In the afternoon, we went inside the venue and were able to watch Howard's soundcheck. He was really lovely to the fans that had made the journey (as usual, some from countries in Europe) and took the time to come and have a chat, saying he hoped we enjoyed the show. I even met Howard's dad, who was in the bar having a drink, and had my photo taken with him, sitting on his lap!

Howard sang some of his songs, which he had written himself, including my favourite 'Speak Without Words', and ended with the Take That anthem 'Never Forget'. Unfortunately, he never did get the record deal or release his music, and a few months later he closed his fan club.

10

CYBER GARY AND THE PARKINSON SHOW

In the weeks that followed the meetings at the Townhouse, I continued to create and update my Gary Barlow website. It wasn't that great a website but, since I had fairly regular contact with Gary, I could provide recent unseen photos and information from my trips to meet him and it did bring me into contact with his online community of fans. One night, one of them kindly told me about a retro Messenger-style chat application called 'Mirc' that Gary's fans used to chat with each other in a channel called 'Gary'. She also told me that Gary himself logged in to talk to his fans, which I did find very hard to believe. Nonetheless, it was worth a try and I soon became one of about twenty or thirty girls across Europe, watching and waiting for another visit from Gary.

No more than a week or two after I had first joined, I saw Gary log in for the first time. Using the nickname 'Jimbo', he caused quite a frenzy within the channel; lots of questions were fired at him but he seemed very slow to actually respond to anything. I had set my nickname as 'Lotterygirl' so that Gary would recognise me and, sure enough, he typed 'Hey Lotterygirl' and asked if it was my first time in the channel. I was a bit dubious as to whether this was actually Gary or not, but over the next couple of weeks whoever this was logged in a few more times using nicknames such as 'SC' and 'Gadget'. This person definitely seemed to have Gary's sense of humour, as one evening he used his status as a channel operator to kick me out of the channel and upon my return asked if I had any bruises!

He never actually responded to my request for a private chat, though. If he had, then I could have asked some more probing questions to see if it was really him. Things went quiet on the channel through the winter, although I did receive some previous chat transcripts from other users in which Gary had sent photos taken in the grounds of his house, including some of the swans in his lake to prove it really was him. He had also revealed that he was to become an uncle when his brother Ian and wife Lisa were expecting their first son, Lewis. One cheeky user typed, 'Well, there is one brother that knows where it hangs!'

When he started logging into the channel again in January 1999, we talked about his upcoming performance and interview on the *Parkinson* show. He hadn't been on television for quite some time and, in his absence (and following Robbie's meteoric rise to fame), he had started to receive some rather negative press. I asked if he would be able to get me into the show's recording at the BBC TV Centre in Wood Lane and he said that he would try, but that he would have a lot on his mind that day and was already feeling nervous about it. During this conversation he asked me if Lorraine would be coming, though he referred to her as 'Blondie'. I told him that she was now engaged and living in Oxford.

The day of the *Parkinson* recording arrived and I desperately tried to obtain some tickets, even calling the show's producer and director, but to no avail: they simply didn't have any left. I resorted to calling Jez, who offered to help get me into the BBC – but at a price. Following my Lottery win, he was now looking to charge me for information and help in all matters Gary! On the day of the *Parkinson* recording, I went to the BBC studios at the time Jez had told me he was going to drop Gary off and awaited his call. When he did call, he told me to go and wait on a nearby street at a particular time and that he would come and pick me up. I waited for him and he arrived in the black Mercedes and told me to lie down in the back as we returned to the BBC. At a security check he said that he was driving Gary Barlow and we were granted entry. After we had parked up, I gave him the £200 fee and he gave me his security pass so that I could get into the building. Having been to the BBC a few times before, I knew my way round and decided to go and get a drink and sit down for a while before I figured out how to get into the *Parkinson* studio itself.

In the canteen where I had ended up, I recognised a few of the people sitting nearby as crew from *The Big Breakfast*. With

WELCOME TO BBC TELEVISION CENTRE

No: 254625

THURSDAY

2 1 JAN 99
Valid for day of issue only

BBC

VISITOR PASS

My BBC pass courtesy of Jez!

nothing to lose, I went over, said hi and asked if they worked on the show; they did, and we began chatting. They seemed really down to earth and so I was honest about my reasons for being there in the hope that they could help me. Together, we hatched a cunning plan that they would say that I was there on work experience and get me into the *Parkinson* studio. One of them was elected to guide me through to the studio, and, as we did so, we went through some sort of control room, where Michael Parkinson himself was perched on the corner of a desk, having a discussion with a producer, and we said hello to each other! Next, I was on the studio floor, where I was introduced to a cameraman as a 'girl on work experience' and was told that I could stand at the side and watch the show being recorded. Just before the start of the show, I was offered a spare seat in the front row; it seemed fate was really on my side again that day!

Gary's interview was really funny, with a clever dig at Robbie over his cocaine use, arguing that he wouldn't want to take a drug that 'drains your bank balance and makes your penis small'! He closed the show with his brand-new song 'Stronger', the first time it had ever been heard. As the studio audience began to exit towards the back, my pass allowed me on to the stage floor, where I congratulated Gary on a great performance and told him that the song was really good. He asked me how I had got in, but I just told him that I was good at it. We walked off down the corridor with his manager, but, as he headed for his dressing room, I went to wait for him in the foyer.

Soon after, he emerged and came over to me and, while playfully tapping my leg with his foot, asked where my friend was. 'I told you already,' I responded, and he replied, 'Oh yeah, Oxford.' At this moment I knew for sure that I had actually been chatting to Gary on the Internet and not some clever impostor, so I smiled cheekily and said, 'So it is you then,' in a sort of Batman/Bruce Wayne revelation, at which he smiled and then looked away.

His manager came over and then it was time for Gary to leave. I went out to rejoin my other friend, Tracy (who I had met a few times at Gary-related events and had now begun to spend more time with in Lorraine's absence), who was waiting by the gates for me. As I recounted the details of my evening and how I had managed to get in, she couldn't believe how lucky I had been and she said that she wished she could have spoken to Gary too. I told her there was still time yet as I knew exactly where Gary was off to next, courtesy of Jez!

Excitedly, we returned to her car and, although I had already seen and spoken to Gary twice that day and worried about what he would think seeing me again, my friend had not been as lucky and so off we drove to a nearby recording studio in London's trendy Notting Hill Gate. On arrival, we saw Gary's musical director Mike Stevens, who stopped to chat to us, but after a couple of hours I decided that I should leave. Having already seen Gary, he would surely think that I had completely lost the plot, had I waited outside a studio in the dark and cold for him too! I called a taxi, but, before it arrived, out walked Gary from the studio. Tracy called his name.

'Fucking hell, you scared me!' he said, startled and laughing, probably not expecting to see anyone that late.

As we hugged, I told him that I didn't mean to be there and that I had called a taxi – I felt like an idiot. But he told me not to feel like that and that it was OK. We talked more about his *Parkinson* interview and his new song, and then thankfully my cab arrived so that I didn't look like a liar, and I said, 'Told you I was leaving!' and off we both went.

One week later, on 28 January, Gary logged into the Mirc channel again. Of course, this time I knew it was him: we chatted for a bit and I told him that I was on a diet; he said that he was too and both of us moaned about how hard it was to stick to it. I also told him that I was trying to quit smoking but he told me not to bother and that smoking was too good to give up! There was a lovely girl on the channel, who lived in Argentina, called Romy who I became friends with and chatted to, while waiting for Gary's random appearances. She was always very envious of how I got to meet Gary all the time and wished that she could see him as much, too. I offered to take Gary a letter from her if she typed it out and sent it in an email to me, and, when a couple of days later a friend told me that Gary was recording at the Sarm West studios, I took it along in an envelope to give to him.

With Lorraine happy and settled in her new relationship and living in Oxford, I once again met up with Tracy for the mission to see Gary at the studios. We sat outside for about an hour and then Gary pulled up in his brand-new Porsche and parked on the corner. I commented on his new car that he was clearly delighted with and then I gave him the email from Romy and we spoke for a while about the late-night Internet chats and some of the regulars in the channel. We posed for yet more photos together, and kept joking about doing 'one more for luck', and I was just glad to be getting another warm hug from him.

When I got home, I put the photos on my low-tech website and excitedly told everyone in the channel (especially Romy) about my day. While chatting later on that night, Gary logged in and this time he made a point of mentioning that he had seen me earlier and jokingly accused me of scratching his brand-new car!

A few days later, when he logged into the channel again, he mentioned to everyone that he had a new hobby. I had spoken to Jez recently and knew that Gary had taken up tennis and so I couldn't resist jumping in and typing 'Tennis'.

Gary typed, 'How do you know?' I remained silent and so he typed, 'Spooky' and we left it at that.

I am sure that after all those years of being in Take That, followed by a hugely successful solo career and seeing fans turn up in all manner of places and knowing all sorts of things, he had given up trying to figure it all out! Over the last few nights in the channel, I had also been made a channel operator and this gave me the power to kick Gary out, which no one else had ever dared do – until now. I decided that it was time to get him back for kicking me out the very first time that he saw me in there and so I booted him right out! The other girls were none too happy that I had ejected the prized member but I knew that he would come back. When he returned, I asked him if *he* had any bruises but he typed, 'It's OK, you know I like it rough!' As always, Gary knew exactly what to say to get me back.

He also mentioned the play that Jason was about to do in London and asked if anyone was going to see it. I said that I had tickets and was going tomorrow, so he said that he would log back in to find out how it went. The next day I did indeed make the short trip to the King's Head Theatre in Islington to see Jason in his new play *Gob*.

The theatre was tiny and was really just a room at the back of a pub. All the die-hard Take That fans gathered in the King's

Head during the day and in the afternoon Jason walked through the pub and out to the theatre. How life had changed for him from the days when two minders would be needed just to get him from a building into a car!

In fact, publicly things had been very quiet for Jason since Take That ended. Instead of trying to launch a solo career in music as the others had done, Jason had taken some time to reflect and travel before concentrating on acting. Despite managing to secure himself a part in the Lynda La Plante drama series *Killer Net*, in which he played a DJ, by and large

Jason poses with his fellow actors after performing in *Gob*, February 1999.

Jason had chosen to take a step back and enjoy the freedom that not being in the public eye could bring, so this was a rare opportunity to see him again.

I thought that Jason's performance was really good and it was a lovely experience to see him in such an intimate environment. We all listened intently and I found that the girls (some had flown in from Italy too) politely saved the screaming and calling his name until the end. Outside the theatre I had my picture taken with him but he said that he was in a rush to get away and didn't spend that much time

Jason after his performance in *Gob*.

with the fans that had come to see him. As promised, Gary logged into the chat room later that night to ask what I had thought about Jason and I filled him in on the day's events.

Despite the frequent visits, after that things went quiet in the chat room and so I called Jez to find out where Gary was. He told me that he had gone to New York with Dawn and the next day it was reported in a newspaper that they had got engaged in the restaurant of the Four Seasons hotel after Dawn had picked out her engagement ring from Tiffany's.

.On my birthday at the end of February, I unexpectedly received something rather wonderful from Gary myself – a birthday card! It read, 'To Claire, Happy Birthday, love Gary'. At first, I was a bit puzzled because Gary did not have my home address and then Tracy called to say that she had sent the card to Gary at Delamere Manor, explaining when my birthday was and asking him to write in it and send it at the appropriate time. It was a lovely idea, and one that had worked so well – and it was very sweet of Gary to have obliged!

Things went even quieter after that; we didn't see him in the channel and there wasn't much else going on until May, when I heard he would be attending the Pride of Britain awards at the Dorchester hotel in London. I went along and managed to get inside, where stars such as the Spice Girls, Michael Owen and Sir Paul McCartney were wandering around, but when I saw Gary he was on his mobile phone and was walking with Dawn at his side. It didn't feel right to talk to him again, and, since I now had long hair extensions, it was quite easy just to turn my head as he walked past so he wouldn't notice me. Up until then, opportunities to see him had been few and far between, but, with the upcoming release of his new single, things were only going to get better.

My birthday card surprise from Gary.

11

A PERIOD OF INSANITY

Through Tracy, I had met a whole bunch of other Take That fans willing to devote a substantial amount of time to tracking down and going to meet them. From these girls I learned how to find out flight information so that we could go to see Gary at Heathrow airport. Gary normally flew with British Airways and had to use his real name as he was travelling with his passport. The girls told me they would wait until midnight and then call the British Airways telephone number. After this time, calls were diverted to offices in the United States, and over there no one had really heard of Gary Barlow so suspicions were not aroused by the mention of his name. From there, all they had to do was ask to check their flight reservation, give the number of a flight that they suspected Gary might be on and check the name. Sometimes the operator would say that it said 'Mr' and either they would say they were male with a high-pitched voice before hanging up or they would admit that it was a mistake and ask for it to be changed to 'Mrs'. I wonder how many times Gary checked in for a flight, only to find that according to British Airways he was now a woman!

In June 1999, as Gary began his promotions for 'Stronger', the first track to be taken from his second album *Twelve Months, Eleven Days*, we caught up with him at Heathrow as he arrived to take a flight to Rome. He had been interviewed recently and had revealed how much he loved Formula One car racing and how he had been to the Grand Prix a couple of times. I thought that it would be a nice gift for him to drive round Silverstone in a Formula One car and so I bought a gift pack and took it to the airport to surprise him.

I asked him first if he had ever done it before or if he had heard of it and he said no. When I showed him the gift, he was really happy, even kissing my cheek three times to say thank you! I told him that I had been at the Le Mans 24-hour race the previous year and how I thought the roar of the engines was sexy and he agreed, saying it was 'fucking brilliant'! I was glad Gary had liked my gift, though I don't know whether he ever used it.

A week later, he was scheduled to do a live interview and performance on *GM:TV* and so the little gang that made up his hardcore group of fans all met at ITV's London Television Centre on the banks of the River Thames near Waterloo. It was incredibly early, but on arrival we were delighted that, with it being a lovely sunny day, they had set up a studio area outside by the river and they were going to present the show from there, meaning we could all watch as it went out live. Gary came wandering over at some point, wearing a green stripy top, and commented on what a beautiful day it was, though he also moaned at how early he had had to get up that morning. We told him that we had all been up very early too just to come and see him!

Tracy congratulated him on his recent engagement to Dawn (which was the mature, sensible thing to do). I, however, chose to be characteristically stupid and, as Gary looked at

Gary waiting to be interviewed live on *GMTV*, June 1999.

me, I just smiled, but somehow I could not bring myself to congratulate him. It was quite an awkward moment, like he was waiting for me to say it, one of those moments in time that seem to go on for minutes but really it was probably only seconds. I really wish that I had just congratulated him and again it's one of those cringe-worthy moments that I regret and would like to go back and change.

We enjoyed the rest of the morning and even chatted to drummer Chris Dagley again as they waited to (pretend to) play live while Gary performed his new song. Afterwards, we posed for more pictures together and then we said that we would see him the following night at his gig at the G.A.Y. at London's Astoria.

The next day we queued up at the Astoria, looking forward to the mini concert Gary was giving at the famous gay nightclub in Charing Cross. Once inside, we began drinking and dancing, even making temporary friends with quite a few guys in there, who were also excited to see Gary. By the time he came on stage late in the evening, we were all already drunk, but had an absolutely fantastic time as he played his new song 'Stronger' and an old Take That hit, 'Relight My Fire'.

When he finished, we rushed round to the back of the club, where a car waited for Gary to leave and Dawn was sitting inside. There were quite a few girls pushing and shoving by the tiny stage door and, when Gary left, there were hands reaching out all over him as he battled his way to the car. A newspaper reported afterwards that the gig had been half-empty and when Gary played club-goers had gone off to the bar to get a drink. I had been there and this was not an accurate write-up of the night at all. The club was full of guys and eager girls and the atmosphere had been electric, especially during 'Relight My Fire'. I couldn't believe what the tabloids were starting to do to Gary – it all seemed so unfair.

Now that I was getting information about his flights, and as promotions for his new song intensified, it seemed as though I was going to see him almost every day! The way that he was being brought down only made me want to be there more to show my undying support. I had no job and my whole life seemed to have become about one man. I wasn't the only one; I had a good group of friends, both close by and online, who shared similar passions and we all encouraged each other to meet up and to do more. It became hard knowing where Gary was (with a constant stream of information from many sources) and not going there to see him, especially since he gave us so much attention when we did see him. It all just came together to be a complete period of insanity.

At Heathrow again, three days after the G.A.Y. gig, there we were again chatting to Gary as he returned from a brief trip to Scotland. We even showed him our photos from the show and, if we came to one where his head was missing or something, he would sarcastically say, 'Oh yeah, love, that's a good one!'

As we walked outside towards the car that was waiting to collect him, Gary explained to me what he had been doing that day, describing his trip up to Scotland as a 'quick in and out', which made me laugh. I apologised, saying that I had a dirty mind and he leaned in to me to say, 'Yes, I know you have!' Well, that certainly shut me up! I was rendered speechless for the next few minutes as a couple of others continued the conversation. The way in which it was said, delivered deep and husky into my right ear, drove me wild; once again Gary had knocked me off-balance in a way that only the two of us knew about. Just before he got into the car he squeezed my arm and smiled; I think he knew what he had done to me. Then he was off again, leaving me breathless.

On 2 July, I went off to Heathrow again, this time not only to see Gary but also to pick up a Portuguese friend that I had met over the Internet called Claudia. She had timed her flight to coincide with Gary's so that she could hopefully get to speak to him at baggage claim! I had arranged for Claudia to stay with me and I had got her tickets for some upcoming UK promotional stuff. She came out at arrivals pretty much alongside Gary, so there I was greeting her with a big hug, while Gary stood close by observing. We all got into one of those huge lifts at the airport, quite a few of us squashed inside, and then we walked with Gary again to his car. We had some photos taken with him – including one of me, Gary and my new friend Claudia! As we posed, Gary told us that he was off to the MTV studios in Camden to record an interview and that he had to leave because he was running a bit late. We hadn't known about this and as I now had Claudia with me, who never normally got to see Gary, I said that we could drive there.

A couple of hours later, we were standing on a street opposite the studios feeling the heat of the gloriously sunny

Gary arriving at the *MTV Select* studios, July 1999.

day. When Gary left the building, he came once again to talk to the assembled fans and then noticed that I was one of them and gave me a look of 'Haven't I already seen you today?' I just smiled, feeling ever more embarrassed that my obsession was clearly growing way out of control!

The next day, Claudia and I headed to Finsbury Park for the Mardi Gras festival, formerly known as 'Pride'. I managed to blag my way into the VIP area and wandered around for a while but there was no sign of Gary so I went back out to join my friends. We made our way down to the stage for Gary's performance and, even though there were plenty of cheers, we noticed a distinct lack of enthusiasm from the crowd. How the manipulation of the media machine was finally working, it seemed! There was Gary Barlow, one-fifth and later one-quarter of Take That, magnificent voice and unquestioned song-writing ability, and yet the media seemed determined to bring him down and we asked ourselves why. Was it that they genuinely didn't like his new material? Did there have to be a winner and a loser in the battle between Williams and Barlow? Whatever it was, it was very sad to see a man like Gary, a man we felt we knew on a personal level, being treated in this way. Wasn't there enough room in British music for both Gary and Robbie?

One thing we had been waiting for was his second solo tour that had now been postponed twice while he took time out to complete his second album. As the shows had been postponed, the people with tickets were entitled to a refund, and, as Gary's popularity dwindled, so too did the number of people coming to his concerts. We were worried the tour would be cancelled altogether if things got any worse, but calls to the record company reassured us that it would still be going ahead.

The next day I waited for Gary's brand-new official website to come online. On a recent second appearance on *GM:TV* – one I had purposefully missed as I worried what Gary would be thinking of me – Chris Healey had asked Tracy for our names so that Gary could thank us personally on his new website. When it finally came online, there it was in black and white, a thank you to his 'regular crew' and my name in the fairly short list of people – his stalkers, if you like! You might think that I would be over the moon at the special mention but it made me realise that I had never started out with a burning ambition to be Gary's number-one fan. It was just that the things that had happened between us, especially on that first tour, had sent me on a never-ending quest for another 'moment' with him and I didn't seem able to stop myself. I did manage to stay away from the crowded London Party in the Park taking place in Hyde Park that same day but had Claudia fill me in on the details when she got back to my flat, where I had been following the live TV coverage.

Soon afterwards, and with Claudia still in tow, we travelled to the MTV studios in Leicester Square where Gary was appearing on Donna Air's afternoon show, *MTV Select*. We met up with some friends at a café just outside the studios – Tracy was there, and a few girls from Germany – and we kept watch for Gary's arrival. I had a couple of glasses of wine in the sunshine and then his car pulled around the corner and I went over to say hello to him again.

When he saw me, he called me 'Clur'. It was the first time he had done so and it felt really nice. We talked about the Party in the Park and how, during an interview backstage, the presenter accidentally referred to Gary's prized 'Stormtrooper' suit from *Star Wars* as a 'Super Trooper' outfit. I said I had been watching at home and found it hilarious, and he was laughing as he remembered it. He told me he had been online later that day on the Party in the Park website for an online chat but hadn't been able to work it out. 'Doesn't surprise me!' I said cheekily and he replied, 'Thanks very much, love!'

As he signed a few autographs and had his picture taken, we kept chatting and, afterwards, Claudia said that it was only me that he really spoke to and that she could see we got on well with each other. I simply told her that I had seen him so many times that I felt relaxed enough to chat to him and I had more things to say now than 'I love your album'.

Later that day, I spoke to Jez again and he told me of a location in London that Gary was going to first thing in the morning for a photo shoot. I debated whether or not to go: it didn't quite feel right, but I had Claudia with me and this would be a great chance for her. She asked me to come with her as she wasn't familiar with London and this wasn't a major site, but a small street in Hackney.

And so I gave in, and the next day there we were, making the journey to Holywell Lane, EC2, to see Gary again – and it turned out to be a big mistake. When his car came round the corner driven by Jez, I felt my stomach lurch; I instinctively knew that I wasn't supposed to be there. Gary started the conversation with: 'Bloody hell! You're keen, twice in two days!' and I wanted the ground to swallow me up. I tried to recover by explaining that I was there to show Claudia where to go as she didn't know London that well, but I knew Gary by now and I knew he wasn't best pleased. Don't get me wrong, he was still very pleasant – he always is – but inside I just *knew*.

For a while I waited and then I called Jez, who confirmed my suspicions. He told me that when Gary had seen us standing there he had fumed, 'How the fuck did they find out about this?' and I felt completely awful. I told Claudia that I was going to go home and she said she would stay and meet me later. Apparently, when Gary left the building hours later he had been in a much more upbeat mood and he even asked Claudia, 'Where's Clur?' She explained to him that I had gone home. Hopefully, that garnered me a tiny bit of respect back!

Three days later, and with Claudia back in Portugal, it was time to go to the ITV studios on the Thames again for the chart show *CD:UK*. I was on the guest list courtesy of Matthew (from *The Funky Bunker*), and Lorraine even made the trip from Oxford. When Gary arrived, Jez flashed the car headlights at us and Gary waved, although this was not to be such a happy day. Inside the studio, Gary sang 'Stronger', but it had just been revealed that, despite being a brand-new single from an unreleased album, it had only made chart position number fifteen. We danced and clapped live on ITV to show our appreciation anyway, but it was true to say that this was not good news for Gary. Outside the studios, we bumped into the drummer Chris Dagley again, who was also having a very bad day as his car had just been clamped!

Three days later, I was once again guest-listed by Matthew, this time for Channel 5's *Pepsi Chart Show*, where Gary was to perform 'Stronger'. I went along with Tracy and we missed him arriving as we had chosen to queue at the audience entrance to get a good position inside at the front of the stage. After he had performed, we went to sit in a bar next door, as we had found out that Gary was to walk through there on his way to the car. We sat and drank some wine, while keeping an eye out for Gary to come up the steps into the bar area. Outside, quite a lot of girls had gathered to see Gary, more than was usual at this point, and, when he came up the stairs and over to speak to us, I warned him there was quite a crowd outside.

He didn't have security any more, only Chris Healey, and so I offered to help out by being his temporary bodyguard. As I did so, I thrust my chest out towards him so as to prove I could beef it up and he gave me the most wide-eyed look yet! He thought for a moment and then said, 'Come on then!' and so we walked towards the exit. Once outside, the screaming began and there was such an incredible noise accompanied by blinding camera flashes. Girls were pushing and shoving to get closer to Gary and a table was overturned next to me, which somehow hit my thumb, twisting it back. We reached the car and Gary quickly ducked down inside and then turned to me and smiled before closing the door and driving off. I wondered what it must have felt like for them during the Take

That days in crowds fifty times bigger and more ferocious than this, after having had just a small taste of what it feels like to walk out into something like that.

A whole month passed before I saw Gary again. I had been busy packing up my flat in London as I had decided to move down to Brighton and had found a gorgeous little flat with a balcony just off the seafront. I felt as though I had done meeting Gary to death and, when I found out that he was going to be flying from Heathrow on 14 August, I seriously

Gary joking around with Eileen at Heathrow Airport, July 1999.

considered whether or not to go. I was chatting to Romy at the time and she told me to flip a coin! I picked tails to go and heads to stay at home and proceeded to throw four tails in a row! Not only that, but, as I did so, 'How Deep is Your Love' came on the radio – you can't really argue with that!

When Gary arrived at Heathrow, he gave me a hug, as always. He noticed my perfume and recognised that I was wearing Thierry Mugler's 'Angel'. I asked him how he knew and he said that he had the male version called 'Amen' – and that he also had the underwear too! As we walked together into the terminal, someone nearby wolf-whistled and shouted, 'Hey, sexy!' I turned and thanked the person, even though the comment was not meant for me, of course, and Gary was laughing as he said, 'Must be the perfume!'

We chatted for a while and I told him about my new flat in Brighton and how there were lots of antique shops down there that he would love (Gary was into antiques at the time). Then, when he had to leave, he gave me a hug, kissed my cheek and said, 'See you later, angel.'

The next time I saw him was just over a week later at Silverstone in Northamptonshire for a one-day music and racing event called 'Summerfest'. Climbing high up on a hill nearby, we could see into the backstage area and waved to Chris Dagley, who was chatting to Chris Healey just below. Gary performed a few songs and spotted us dancing and cheering as always and gave us a huge smile.

On 11 September, with two other members of Gary Barlow's 'regular crew', Eileen and Lucy, I went to the BBC TV studios in

Wood Lane for yet another of his *National Lottery Show* appearances, this time to promote 'For All That You Want', the second (and last) single to be released from *Twelve Months, Eleven Days*. While out shopping earlier in the week, I had spotted a big lollipop in the shape of a light sabre that also glowed and, knowing Gary's *Star Wars* obsession, I decided to buy it and take it along to the *Lottery Show*. Quite a few girls were standing outside waiting for Gary to leave but we did manage to grab him for a few moments and give him the gift that he found very funny and he said he would have a lot of fun with it.

At the end of September, we knew that Gary was doing some rehearsals for an upcoming show at Sheffield's Boardwalk and I tried to find out where they were taking place. On the morning of 27 September, Gary's 'regular crew' took part in *The Big Breakfast*'s campaign to have his new single 'For All That You Want' put on the Radio One playlist, as there was a rumour that he would be there himself to perform the song outside the Radio One building. We had to hold banners and march around, until eventually Zoë Ball came out to talk to someone from the show she once presented about why Radio One were not playing the song. She said that, although she really liked Gary, she thought perhaps the song 'just wasn't that good'.

Tired of marching around, we sat in the car and listened to the Radio One broadcast, waiting for them to play the song, but they stuck to their guns and continued to leave Gary off their playlist. Gary, of course, didn't show up and so our attention turned back to the rehearsals he was doing for the Sheffield show. I remembered Jez telling me about a rehearsal venue in Putney that Gary had used before and we drove there on the off chance this could be the one.

We arrived at the Ritz Studios on Disraeli Road and parked up. But we hadn't been there very long before, amazingly, we saw Chris Dagley walking down the road and we stopped him for a chat. He told us that this was indeed where they were rehearsing and that Gary hadn't arrived yet. Everyone was astounded we had got it right as there were so many places that he could have been! What was more amazing was that, within ten minutes of our arriving and parking up, Gary had driven round the corner to park and we were waiting for him to walk around the corner to the studios.

He was dressed very casually and I don't think he had expected to see anybody as he strolled around the corner. We were all just as surprised to be having this unexpected encounter with him too – I mean, there is lucky and then there's damn unbelievably lucky! After the usual hug, I commented that he smelled very nice and he told me that he was wearing the aftershave by Yohji Yamamoto, and then Lucy looked down and saw that she was wearing the same trainers as Gary! They laughed, and we told him about our morning at the Radio One studios and all the protesting that had gone on there. He said that he had to crack on with his rehearsals and we told him that we were all going to Sheffield for the show on Saturday.

Despite being incredibly tired from getting up early to come to London to support *The Big Breakfast* campaign, we decided to go and get something to eat and then return to the Ritz Studios to wait for Gary to leave. By the time he did, it was dark and we chatted for a while before he walked off down the road towards his car. I then remembered something that I had wanted to tell him and so I ran off after him. It was just me and him now and I told him that I had listened to the new album (though it hadn't been released at that point, I had received it on tape from a contact) and that I thought 'Lie to Me' was an absolutely amazing track and wondered why the record company had not chosen to release that particular song. Gary seemed to agree, but suggested they had decided to go for more up-tempo tracks to get away from his ballad image; even during Take That, the more up-tempo songs had been cover versions. He then told me that he was doing a small show in Bristol in two days' time and would be playing the new songs there, so said that I would be there and off he went again.

As promised, I turned up to support Gary at the Wickham Theatre in Bristol with Tracy and Eileen and we waited in the cold for Gary to arrive. The theatre was very small and, had it not been for Gary, even us diehard fans would not have known that he was going to play there that evening. When he arrived, he looked tired but posed with us for some photos before going inside. A short while later, Chris Healey came out with a pass for all of us so that we could get inside later and enjoy the show. We were really happy about that and thought it a very kind gesture on Gary's part. Once inside the theatre, we saw Chris Dagley again and chatted to him about the rehearsals and the tour that was due to start in just over two months. He told us that everyone had just ordered lots of pizza backstage and that Gary had gone mad on pizzas recently, ordering them whenever they were rehearsing or playing somewhere.

He went off to enjoy his dinner and soon we went inside the actual performance area and sat in the front row waiting for Gary to come out and play. This was the first time I had seen him perform songs from his new album live and, as I had received my 'illegal' copy some days before, I already knew all of the words, something Gary found most puzzling as he watched me sing along with him, songs that I really shouldn't have even heard yet! At the end, we thanked him for giving us the passes to get in and he told us that we were very welcome.

Soon it was Saturday, and the long drive up to Sheffield to see Gary perform at the Boardwalk, which would provide us with a nice taster of his second solo tour that was getting ever nearer. We arrived in the afternoon and I bypassed the steadily growing queue that was forming outside by telling security that I was the drummer's girlfriend and went inside with Tracy, who had driven up with me. The venue was very small and we saw that Gary and his musicians were doing a soundcheck on the stage and having a general mess around before the show later. We sat down and watched them rehearse and laughed at Gary's many jokes as he kept everyone amused while they did their practice. They were going over some of the songs and trying slightly different arrangements and we would even show our approval if something sounded particularly good with a thumbs-up.

After rehearsing, they all went backstage and we had a few drinks to pass the time. When the security team looked ready to open the doors to the swelling queue outside, we went to the front of the stage to bag our places and places for our friends, who were just about to enter. Once the doors were finally opened, there was a mad dash of people surging down to the stage, and later we noticed that Gary's mother, father, brother and sister-in-law were all there to support him too.

Gary plays a selection of songs from his new album at The Boardwalk, Sheffield, in October 1999.

The show went down really well, not least because the room was filled with dedicated Gary Barlow fans that had travelled from all over Europe just to see him that night. It made for a really good atmosphere and was very supportive, considering what Gary had been through recently. At the end, he stopped and posed for photos and signed autographs with loads of the fans, and I stood by the bar watching as I felt I had seen him so much already and that the others, who don't see him so often, should spend the time with him.

When he was about to leave, he walked through and then spotted me by the bar; we said hello and I told him that it was a really good show and that we would see him again soon. Not wanting to waste a perfectly good night in Sheffield, we proceeded to hit the town and, on a high from the concert, we had the most amazing night, joining up with a group of guys in fancy dress and doing a bar crawl with them! It wasn't all standing in the cold or waiting around to see Gary; there was a great bunch of girls that had become true friends and there was always so much fun to be had on our adventures.

The one we looked forward to the most, of course, was Gary's tour – I was literally counting down the days when I could hopefully spend more than five or ten minutes with him again and get into a good conversation in the hotels. Later that October, we saw him at Heathrow airport and this time we had taken him a giant Chupa Chups lollipop. Such was his confessed love of confectionery that we often took him sweets to keep him happy! I told him the lollipop was a bit too big for my mouth and he asked me if I was sure about that! He asked if we were coming to the airport the next day before he took his flight to Holland, but we said no, as we had no plans to.

Afterwards, we considered it and the next day we all met up again at Heathrow! We watched people arrive for every flight to Holland that day and, as the event there was a pop awards show, we saw bands like 5ive and Westlife turning up to check in for their flights and even new boy band Northern Line. There was no sign of Gary, though, and later we were told by a member of staff he had been on the earliest flight at around 7 a.m. and that we had missed him.

Quite a substantial amount of time passed before I saw Gary again, a good six weeks, which compared to the past year was a *huge* gap! We had found out that he was once again rehearsing at the Ritz Studios in London in the run-up to the tour and one night we went down there to see how it was going. I think there had been so much threat to this tour that meant so much to us that we wanted to see for ourselves that rehearsals were indeed taking place and that it was still going ahead!

That night, we saw some new faces: alongside the familiar ones of Chris Dagley and Bernie Smith, there was a new guitarist and bass guitarist and a percussionist who looked uncannily like Jonathan Ross! Chris told us they had even given him the nickname 'Wossy'. When Gary left the studios, he put the window down at the back of the car and I leaned in to kiss his cheek. With only one week to go before the tour, I asked if he was nervous and he admitted that he was a little bit, but that things were going well. This tour was originally set to take place in autumn 1998 and had been postponed to spring 1999, and then further to winter 1999. We had waited and waited, and then waited some more, but now it was finally here: months of anticipation and planning had come together for those two weeks with Gary on his second solo tour.

12
TWO WEEKS, TWO DAYS

Preparations for Gary's tour had been going on for some time; there was the ferocious diet to get down to a size 12, the hundreds of pounds spent on clothes, make-up and other tour essentials, the gorgeous black diary containing driving routes and maps all neatly printed and secured inside next to tickets and hotel information, trips to the salon for manicures, pedicures, haircuts and more – even my new car received some pampering when I sent it off for a full valet service the night before we left.

Although we were meeting up with Eileen and Lucy along the way, Tracy was to be my tour partner this time, sharing the journeys and hotel rooms as we disappeared into a little bubble of time, encapsulated in the unreality of the tour for the next two weeks and two days. We had tickets for every single concert, of which there were 11, and planned to stay in every hotel along the way.

The day before the first concert on 7 December 1999, we set off for Cornwall – we had an inkling Gary would be there a day early for final rehearsals and also it was a long drive from Brighton and we wanted to get it out of the way. As we headed West, Tracy called Mark from Gary's fan club and he told us 'they' were already in Cornwall, whoever 'they' might be, though things looked promising. Meanwhile, Lucy, who was still at home, was name-checking some of the top hotels in Cornwall and had tracked them down to the Carlyon Bay hotel. Although it was fully booked on that night, she had gone ahead and booked us both rooms for the following evening.

On arrival at the Carlyon Bay, we noticed a small hotel opposite called the Cliff Head and we managed to get a room there for that evening. As the porter helped us with an entire boot full of bags (seats folded flat to help accommodate them), rather puzzled, he asked, 'Just the one night?' and we explained that we were actually away for quite some time.

We spent a few moments freshening up and then excitedly walked the short distance to the Carlyon Bay. Once there, we headed straight to the bar, which was cosy and quiet; we didn't yet recognise anyone so ordered some drinks to help us relax. After a while, I went to the reception and asked the girl there if she would pass on a message to Chris Dagley's room, telling him that we were in the bar if he fancied a drink. I read the word 'trainee' on her name badge and she didn't seem to know what she was doing, so I just went back to sit down again in the bar and told myself to be patient.

It wasn't long before some 'likely suspects', as we called

them, came into the bar. As they were wearing laminated passes and were much younger than the rest of the guests, who seemed at least fifty, we had a strong feeling that they were part of the tour. I walked past them to get a closer look and, sure enough, 'Gary Barlow' was written on their passes. Confirmation was ours and the anticipation rose a little more as we waited and hoped that Gary himself was also at the hotel.

Keyboard player Bernie was next to enter the bar and when he saw us he came over to sit with us, which I thought was very lovely of him and so I offered to buy him a drink. He asked for a pint of bitter shandy, but then said that really he should stick to a half or else he would be very drunk! Just as I was ordering the drinks, in walked Mr Dagley, who also joined us at our table, and, as I had copied some videos for him over the summer, he bought us the round of drinks. We had the band at our table, so thoughts turned to whether or not Gary would join us too! Meanwhile, we quizzed Chris and Bernie about the show; they said they had just come from rehearsals but that they were not giving anything away and we would have to wait until the following night! They did, however, confirm that Gary was there.

When Gary did walk into the bar, I stood up and he walked towards me. All of the excitement had got on top of me and I said, really stupidly, 'Hello, Mr Sexy!' (Oh, just kill me now!) Gary looked at me oddly, but nonetheless we hugged each other and I asked him if he was looking forward to the first show. I have no idea what he replied because in my head I was questioning why I had just greeted him by referring to him as Mr Sexy! He moved closer to Tracy and gave her a hug and she told him to pull up a chair, but he said he had to talk to Chris Healey and the rest of the band and so he went to sit with them instead. Bernie and Chris Dagley stayed with us, though, and so we enjoyed the rest of the evening, chatting to them and downing more and more drinks, as was tour tradition, of course.

A while later, a tired-looking Gary came over and told us that he was going to bed now. He reassured us that he would see us more the next night and he held my hand as he leaned across me to say goodnight to Tracy, then he was gone. We stayed up drinking a good few hours after Gary had gone to bed. In the end, the bar had closed, the shutters were down and still Chris, Tracy and I were sitting in the bar completely paralytic. I tried to get into the swimming pool but thankfully the door was locked and then I said that I couldn't walk any more and ended up crawling along the floor, much to the amusement of the other two, who crouched down to have pictures taken with me. By the time we said goodnight to Chris and staggered over to the Cliff Head and lay down, the entire room was spinning. I felt as though I would be sick but managed to get to sleep without throwing up!

The next morning I woke feeling dreadful, as you can imagine, and ventured down for breakfast, mainly sticking to tea and orange juice. Following this, we packed up the car and drove to the car park opposite and then another porter, this time with a shiny gold trolley, helped us up to another room with all our stuff. We went down to the bar to get some water and memories of the previous drunken night came flooding back, some that I really didn't want to remember! I sat trying to recover and then Chris walked in, also looking the worse for wear, and asked if he could have some of my water to take his painkillers!

In the afternoon, Lucy and Eileen arrived and we told them about the previous night in the hotel and then we all excitedly began getting ready for the show that we had waited for for so long. I did my make-up with one eye on the mirror and one on the window that looked out to the front of the hotel, where I could see the band getting into the tour bus to set off for the show.

Just as excitedly, we met up in the hotel foyer and Lucy drove us to the venue, a mere five minutes' away. We each bought a tour programme and Gary summed up our feelings when he wrote inside the front cover, 'It feels so great to get the show on the road even though at times it seemed the odds were stacked against me.' He finished the message to his fans, 'Thank you for being so patient and for sticking with me. I appreciate you all more than you'll ever know.' The tour programme also doubled as a calendar for the year 2000 and on each page he had inserted pictures of himself with his fans. Then, on the month of July, there I was: a picture that had been taken so long ago at the recording of *Talking Telephone Numbers*!

The new coliseum in St Austell, Cornwall, had quite a pungent smell to it and was a rather small venue. Despite this, only half of the seats had been bought that evening. Chris had told us that Gary had got this venue for free and that, really, it was just a warm-up show. Originally he had been scheduled to begin the tour in Ireland with a show in Dublin and then one in Belfast, but they had been cancelled and replaced with shows in Cornwall and then Ipswich. We had, of course, had no trouble getting good seats for both, with not exactly huge queues of people in a race to get his tickets any more.

The support act was a young lady named Nicole Lacy, whose small white boob tube kept slipping down as she tried to get through her songs! I worried what Gary would make of

Gary performs on his second solo tour.

this rather quiet crowd when he came on to the stage – they were far from the screaming, whistle-blowing audience he had always had before. After Nicole finished, it seemed to take forever for Gary to come on stage and we joked that the dry ice we could see billowing from behind the drum kit was, in fact, Gary smoking ten cigarettes to calm his nerves! Then the music began and Gary sang the first line from the song 'Arms Around Me', which began 'Out of the water', and then during the next few lines he appeared on the stage and saw us immediately in the second row and smiled. His voice sounded amazing and he performed songs from both his solo albums and also a Take That medley in the middle. I felt very sad for him, though – that a man of such enormous talent was playing in a smelly, half-empty venue.

Back at the hotel, we bumped into the band members on the hotel corridor and Bernie asked me to introduce him to my friends, Lucy and Eileen – only in doing so I incurred myself some penalties, as all night we were playing a game in which we had changed all of our names to match the first letter of the place we were in. So, in honour of being in Cornwall, our names were now Connie, Cynthia, Carol and Crystal and, if you were to get a name wrong, you had to down your drink! Down in the bar, I began the night by knocking back two vodka and oranges and then we waited for Gary and everyone else to come down.

When they did, they appeared to be having quite some meeting, chaired by Gary's manager Kristina Kyriacou, so we decided to go to a function room next door where there was a Christmas party going on. We got covered in the paper remnants of exploded party poppers and were thrilled when the DJ played 'Relight My Fire', although none of the partygoers knew that the singer of that particular song was on the other side of the wall! We got some looks when we returned from the party, looking as though we were having an absolute ball – which we were – and then Gary stood up and came over to our table.

He asked us what we thought of the show and we discussed with him the bits that were really good, but also how sad we had felt seeing him perform in such a venue and he agreed that it was weird for him too, especially since during the slower songs the audience actually sat down and listened instead of screaming all the way through. We told him about the support act and how her top had been falling off, and also that she had looked a bit cold, if he knew what we meant! We asked if we could have a group photo with him as a reminder of the first night of the tour and he agreed, moving to sit on the arm of my chair. Eileen mentioned that he smelled nice and he bent his neck down towards me so that I could have a smell as he told us that it was Jean Paul Gaultier.

After the first picture was taken, Gary told me he had done a nice cheesy smile so I said we had to do another one and that he should pull a normal face! He went back to join the band, and while continually slipping up in our name game we got more and more drunk, and with it became louder and louder. Someone brought a 'Sanitised For Your Protection' sticker down from one of the toilets, which I proceeded to stick around my head, and we kept on going back to the party next door – now there was even a male strip show going on!

Once Gary had gone to bed, we went to sit with the band, where we explained our name game, and the boys all took new names too so that they could join in, with Chris becoming Clarke. I was introduced to Dave the guitarist, who was a Pisces like me, so we tagged ourselves as 'Pisces Brother' and 'Pisces Sister'. I also met 'Wossy', who seemed like a really nice guy. At some point, Tracy pulled out her little vibrating spider called Millie – the guys loved it and insisted that at some point during the tour we get them all one.

At 4 a.m., the drinks waitress came over to ask if we wanted any more as she was about to close the bar and we knew that the right thing was to say no. However, as soon as we had, we regretted it and had to go and ask her please for yet another round of drinks. We all took turns to buy rounds of drinks but our bar bill from that night alone topped £100!

As it was nearly 5 a.m., we decided that really we should go to bed, especially with a huge drive to Ipswich the next day. I decided that I needed to get some more tour information from Chris, so Tracy and I hatched a plan to kidnap his room key and the ransom was the details we needed for the rest of the tour. When we walked up to Chris's room with Dave alongside, none of us could walk straight and we kept banging into the walls of the corridor, creating quite some disturbance. As we stood waiting to get into Chris's room, some old guy appeared from the room opposite and told us angrily to keep the noise down. We did, however, find it hard to take him seriously as he was stark naked!

We all piled in, and there on the table was the full tour itinerary called 'The Book of Lies', apparently, as Chris explained, because plans changed quite a lot on tour. We had struck gold and, although Chris protested heavily, I managed to get the book and drunkenly scrawl down all the information on to a hotel notepad. Suddenly there was a knock at the door and Dave, Tracy and I all hid in the bathroom while Chris answered. It was a member of staff complaining that we were making too much noise and sternly warning us to keep it down. With our mission completed, we were free to leave and so we thanked Chris and then went off to our room.

Despite it being so early and our being heavily intoxicated, I proceeded to make calls to some of the hotels on the list to book rooms; however, with Tracy laughing hysterically in the background and me slurring my words, I decided that I should, in fact, leave it until the morning.

When I woke the next day, it felt as though I had only just gone to sleep and I thought that there was no way I could get up. The phone was ringing and Lucy and Eileen wanted to know if we could meet them for breakfast. I don't know how, but somehow I made it down to meet them and I told them that we knew all the hotels for the rest of the tour and that we could book them later on in Ipswich. It was a big rush to get everything packed up and in the car before check-out time and what a horrible feeling to have a seven-hour drive ahead of us too!

Just before we set off, I received a call from Nicky Gray at Globe Artists to say that I had won a competition to meet Gary backstage before the Newcastle show. I didn't feel too lucky – probably not that many people had entered the competition – and, after I hung up, Tracy then received a call from the same woman, telling her that she too had won the chance to meet Gary backstage, this time at Cardiff!

By the time we arrived at the Belstead Brook hotel in Ipswich, we were painfully tired and desperately needed to get some sleep. The band were in the hotel but Gary was not arriving until the following evening as he was filming Ian Wright's new ITV show, *Friday Night's All Wright*, in London, so we decided just to have an early night.

The next evening, having enjoyed a day relaxing at the hotel and walking in the grounds, we gathered in the hotel foyer, this time with another friend called Debbie, and we took a cab to the Ipswich Regent Theatre for Gary's second show. When we got there, we chatted to Chris and he told us that Gary had taken the train there and then a cab to the venue!

The show that evening was so much better than Cornwall, with a much livelier crowd. We were right at the front, having slipped forward from the second row when everyone stood up, and Gary looked so much happier than he had done at the first show. When he introduced his band members, we let off party poppers for them all and, as Bernie played his solo, I began chanting, 'Go, Bernie!' until the entire audience joined in; it was really amazing.

Gary said, 'Seems Bernie has his fan club in tonight!'

Just before the end of the show, we made a dash outside and grabbed a taxi back to the hotel, and arrived minutes before Gary. As he entered the lobby, I gave him a big hug and said how much better that evening had been and he agreed; he had a towel wrapped around his neck and explained that it was keeping his throat warm. He asked us how on earth we had beaten him back to the hotel but we just smiled and then I confessed to him that I had been the one who had started the Bernie chant. We all began walking towards the hotel corridor and, as I held the door open for Gary, I jokingly asked if he was following us. He replied, 'I hope not – I have heard that you lot are way too noisy!' I laughed, remembering the raucous night in Cornwall, and, then as he headed off up some stairs, he said, 'I will see you in the bar later.'

Despite this, and the fact that Gary was indeed in the bar, we didn't speak to him at all that night. Instead, we chatted with Mark, the merchandising guy, and enjoyed a few drinks. The band looked as though they were going to go out as they came into the bar quite dressed up but then they decided to stay, and after Gary had gone to bed we went to sit with Chris and bass guitarist Orefo for a chat. It's odd how, when you're on tour, one night Gary can come and sit at your table with you and the next not say a word, but we always have fun anyway and take the highs with the lows. From our point of view, he is the main focus; however, for Gary, there are a lot more concerns while he is on the road and a lot more people to speak to in the course of any evening. Sometimes, it is merely a case of picking the right table in the bar, one that will end up being close to the table Gary sits at!

The next morning at breakfast, we sat around a large table,

feeling hungover and tired, and watched as some of the band members, also looking tired, sat on a nearby table. We ordered cooked breakfasts and helped ourselves to plenty of fruit juice and tea, and then, just as we were being served with our hot food, Gary walked over to our table.

'Good morning,' I began.

'Fucking hell!' he replied, upon seeing all the delicious food.

'A simple good morning would suffice!' Tracy joked, and we all laughed.

On further inspection of my poached eggs, Gary commented on how good they looked and, for some unknown reason, I replied, 'Yeah, the yolk's all runny and they taste so yummy!'

Gary looked at me strangely and I told him that I had no idea where that had just come from, but maybe I should become a lyricist and could write him a song. (Note to self: learn when to shut up!) As Gary walked off, I felt rather stupid, as you can imagine, and I decided just to go to the room and begin the now very annoying job of packing everything up again, to move on once more.

That day we had another long drive all the way up to Newcastle and I couldn't be late because that evening it was my meeting with Gary backstage!

When we finally arrived at the Malmaison at the Quayside, the band were getting ready to leave for the show and, as we checked in, Gary came down to reception and waved at me and smiled before leaving. I had barely one hour to shower and get ready to go and meet Gary, and I still hadn't eaten anything at all that day since the breakfast at the hotel. I ordered up a bowl of fries and tried to grab a few handfuls before my cab arrived to take me to Newcastle City Hall.

Standing outside the artists' entrance in the cold, smoking a cigarette, I felt very silly. I had met Gary so many times that this would feel rather awkward and when I entered the competition I had anticipated that you could take a friend in with you, but now I had to go in alone.

Once I was inside and Gary had entered the small room that we had been ushered into, he joked, 'Oh, hello, I have never seen you before,' and smiled before saying hello to the other competition winners. I think that he could tell I was nervous and feeling a bit odd because he kept turning to wink at me reassuringly. I gave him a pair of R2D2 socks, his favourite character from *Star Wars*, which he said were wicked and he almost jumped up and down like a child. He then passed them to a member of the team, saying that he definitely wanted to keep them.

I tried to fade into the background a bit, but then one girl asked me to take a picture of her and Gary. I couldn't see through her lens properly and was struggling a bit, and Gary was moaning jokily, 'Come on, Claire!' and looking at me mischievously.

After I finally managed to take the picture, I thrust the camera at Gary and said, 'You bloody try it then!' and even he couldn't do it, so everyone was laughing.

His next trick was to see how much he could embarrass me by telling people in the room, 'Oh, Claire told me this and

Claire told me that,' saying different things that we had spoken about over the last few days, like the support act's top falling down on the first night, to name just one. Of course, people kept looking at me and they must have been a bit puzzled. I moved in for a picture to be taken with Gary and he said in my ear, 'Angel,' and I said back to him, 'Jean Paul Gaultier,' and he told me that Dagley had the same aftershave as him now, so I told him that I knew that, while having a memory of a few nights back, hiding in Chris's bathroom, where a drunken Tracy had sprayed some around!

The organiser then told us that time was up and Gary thanked us all before we left. I watched him as he poked his head round a nearby door, said something and then walked off. When I got there, I saw that it was the canteen and I don't know what he had said, but Wossy stood up from his seat and looked at me, and then he said, 'See you in the bar later!' That did feel kind of cool.

The Newcastle show started very well, with a great audience, but, just as Gary was about to sing 'Forever Love', he sneezed. This worked in his favour, though, as the crowd loved it and thought it was very funny! He told us later that, from then on, he would do that every night to get a laugh. More seriously, something seemed to have gone very wrong midway through the show, when we noticed that some songs had been dropped and others put in, and sensed a bit of tension on the stage. Some of the staff at the City Hall also thought it hilarious to wind Gary up by wearing Robbie Williams's tour T-shirts, which was very lame.

We beat Gary back to the hotel once more and, as we walked through the revolving doors of the hotel, I told him that I was really hungry and was going to order some food, but he looked unhappy and slightly pissed off as he walked quickly to the lifts with manager Chris. The restaurant was full and so I had to order up some food to the room and all the girls were in there with me: Tracy, Lucy, Eileen and Debbie. We played some music and messed around, until some man knocked on the door, telling us to be quiet as he had just come off a transatlantic flight! Nothing could dampen our spirits, though – we were on tour and we loved it!

When we got down to the bar, Gary was already there with the band, and Chris and Dave stood up and gave us a wave. We enjoyed a few drinks and then I became a little bored and wanted to get Gary's attention. I called over the drinks waitress (it was this very hotel where the previous year where Gary had bought drinks for Lorraine and I after I told him about my Lottery win) and I ordered a round of drinks for our table. When she returned with the bill, I told her that this was Gary's round and that she should take the bill to him to sign. The others couldn't believe what I was doing but nonetheless found it very funny. It took a bit of convincing, but in the end she went over to Gary with the bill and pointed over to us and we all nervously watched his reaction. He looked over and frowned, and then stuck his two fingers up and returned the bill over to us! Despite this, my plan worked and Gary left his table and came to sit next to us, although he did warn us sternly before he sat down, 'I will buy you drinks when I *want* to buy you drinks!'

Over the next couple of hours, we engaged in conversation with him, discussing the recently released film *The Blair Witch Project*, and how the grounds of the Ipswich hotel had resembled it. Gary told us that his favourite film that year had been *Sixth Sense* and then of course he launched into more filthy jokes that he loved to tell so much. Tracy had one of her own up her sleeve, though, and she asked Gary, 'If a white stork brings a white baby and a black stork brings a black baby, what brings no baby?' He shook his head and so she told him it was a swallow! He didn't seem to get it, so we cheekily offered to demonstrate – though this was after a few shots of tequila, I might add. Tracy also asked him to guess what she did for a living but he said straight away that she worked for Vodafone, so the band and Gary must have been discussing us at some point for him to know such details.

It was also the same evening when I told Gary that he had a showbiz admirer in the form of Jennifer Aniston but he didn't seem bothered by that at all, even though I thought he would be flattered. After he had said goodnight to us and gone off to bed, we made use of the private lounge upstairs that was reserved for residents who were staying in suites only. We always booked a suite at the Newcastle Malmaison just in case we needed access to the private lounge, although, as far as we knew, Gary never used it. Inside the plush lounge was a stereo system, a touch control panel on the wall operating the lights, an open fire and even a chessboard. We put Gary's second album on and were joined by the tour's merchandising guy to enjoy a few more drinks before we all went off to bed.

The next morning, I woke feeling as though I was still drunk, and I got dressed and went down to the lobby to see what was happening. Some of Gary's fans had gathered in the foyer and outside the hotel, waiting for him to leave. I had planned to go and get my car and pull it up at the front of the hotel to load the luggage but noticed two tour buses were blocking the road there. Instead, I chatted to Judith Holmshaw, one of Gary's most loyal fans, who was sitting in her wheelchair just by the hotel doors. It was a really cold day and she explained that Gary had told her that he would come out to see her last night but had forgotten and that she had been there for quite some time.

Hungover and incredibly thirsty, I made my way back up to my room to get a bottle of water and some chewing gum, and, as the lift doors opened, there stood Gary, wearing sunglasses and carrying a rucksack on his back. 'Oh, God!' I groaned, expressing how rough I felt and knowing that Gary knew why. We hugged and kissed cheeks, and then I told him I had wanted to bring my car around the front of the hotel but some fucking band were staying here and were blocking the way. Of course, I meant his own band, but Gary responded, 'Oh yeah, Earth, Wind and Fire are staying here!' I thought that was very quick-witted and I laughed. I told him that I had been dreaming about him last night but, just as it was getting good, Lucy rang my room and woke me up, making me very annoyed with her! I then apologised, saying that I thought I was still drunk, and so he told me to lay off the tequila next time.

Gary was now in the lift and, every time the doors went to

Gary with Judith Holmshaw and her mother,
Newcastle, December 1999.

close, he had to stick his foot out to stop them while we talked. I told him that Judith was outside and was really cold, and asked how he could have forgotten to go and see her. He looked really guilty and so I told him to just go and give her an extra-special hug to make up for it! He asked me if I was going to Glasgow and I said yes, so he said that he would see me there later. This was good news: that night there was no show so he could have gone home and then flown up the next day, but now we knew we would see him again later.

The drive up to Glasgow was interesting – having missed a

turning, we ended up on some small winding roads and even passed through many small villages like Frosterly and Westgate, each with their own sweet little post offices all dressed up for the seasonal period. The sightseeing, although fun, was not getting us where we needed to go and we were even more frustrated when Eileen called to tell us that Gary had already arrived at the Glasgow Malmaison and was enjoying a coffee in the bar! When we finally arrived, he was still in the bar with Chris but, after a quick hello, we had to drag all of the bags up to yet another room. I felt like I wanted to get on the bed and sleep for a few weeks – all the late nights and long drives had really caught up with me – but you just have to keep going because Gary Barlow is in the bar again!

Eileen overheard dinner plans being made for the band at a restaurant outside the hotel and after they had left I spent some time in the room relaxing and getting ready for another evening in a hotel bar. Once down there, we secured a table and the drinking began again. Soon after, Gary and the band came in and I was happy because the only spare table left was next to us. As one girl approached to take a seat there, Gary told her that he wanted to sit there and I was really thrilled because now I was opposite him and we said our hellos.

Over the next two hours, I had the most wonderful time chatting to Gary that I could ever have imagined. I felt relaxed and as though we were just friends having fun; we talked about our plans for Christmas and New Year, we discussed his career and everything that had happened that year, and his second album and how he felt about it now that it hadn't done so well and had been panned by critics. He thanked his band members for sticking by him, and, as Bernie was sat to my left, I kept ordering him more and more drinks and Gary was telling me off for getting his band drunk, as they had to play the next night. I asked him if there was going to be any sort of end-of-tour party in Cardiff but he said that he wasn't even going to stay over there now; instead, he was going straight home for Christmas. I was gutted to hear that, as I knew it might be my last night with him for a long time, or indeed forever. I told him that I feared I might never see him again and he reassured me by saying that I would definitely see him again. I told him that I hoped so and he said that he hoped so too.

We talked about Howard, who had just become a father to a little girl named Grace, and how he was coping with being a parent. Gary told me that Howard would be coming along to a few shows soon and that I would probably meet him. When we spoke about Newcastle, I realised that Earth, Wind and Fire had actually been staying at the hotel and I explained to Gary that I had laughed so much because I thought he was joking! I asked him if he had kept the R2D2 socks and he said that he had, and to prove it he would wear them on stage soon and give me a little flash.

I was in absolute heaven; I felt that, despite the copious amounts of ridiculous things I had said and done over the years, Gary thought I was all right and that meant a lot. Out of millions of fans worldwide, I never forgot how privileged I was to have the opportunity to spend time with him like that, but like all good things they do have to come to an end. After going to the toilet and returning to find someone that he didn't like in Bernie's seat, Gary went off to join the support act Nicole.

We carried on drinking and having fun anyway. Tracy had some 'Won't Kiss Off' lipstick that she thought would be a good idea to test for Revlon, only her idea was not to test it on us girls, but rather on the band! Amazingly, they agreed and we applied some lipstick to Chris, Dave and Wossy. They had to kiss everyone at the table on the cheek to see if it would last. At some point, Gary decided that he was going to go to bed and he came to say goodnight. I pointed at my cheek in expectation of a kiss and, after receiving one, I requested a 'European'. He said, 'Oooooh!' and then kissed my other cheek.

Soon after, we all decided that we were going to bed too and squeezed into the lift together. When the lift stopped on our floor, we invited everyone into our room, and in they all piled: Tracy, Lucy, Eileen, myself, Chris, Dave and Wossy. I had my video camera in there and I thought it would be funny to make a video, so, while being discreet, I set it to record and left it by the TV. We were all laughing and joking around and we made a deal that the next day we would go to some charity shops in Glasgow and get them all stage shirts for the show. Dave noticed the camera rolling at some point and got up to switch it off, except all he did was turn it towards the wall so there was still audio running. At about 4 a.m., I had to go and sort out the parking on my car as it was liable to get clamped in the morning. Lucy, who hadn't been drinking, came with me to move both her car and mine, and I told her what Gary and I had been chatting about all evening.

As promised, the next day we went into Glasgow shopping and I can honestly say that that day was one of the happiest of my life. Having had so much fun the night before, we were now shopping for stage clothes for the band and looking forward to the Glasgow concert that evening; we even found large orange versions of Tracy's vibrating spider and we bought one for each of the band as they had requested in Cornwall. We stocked up on party poppers to let off again when Gary introduced the band members on stage and found some garish shirts in the British Heart Foundation shop that we wondered if the band would really wear.

Back at the hotel, we called Chris's room and he told us to bring the shirts and spiders to him. He gave us a list of all the room numbers, even Gary's, and said that it would be fine for us to take the spider to him but we decided to give it to him before he left the hotel instead in case he got annoyed. When we delivered the other spiders, we placed them by the door on vibrate mode so they looked as though they were humping the ground and then we would knock on the door and hide around the corner – they all found it very funny.

We went down to the lobby just as they were gathering to leave and spoke to Gary for a while. He too had been out shopping that day and had a couple of posh bags on him. The previous night, he had recommended a few albums to me and I asked if he had been out buying them for me as a Christmas gift. But he told me they were not available in the UK. I said that I felt like I was on a boat as everything was swaying a bit as I walked, and Wossy said, 'I'll have some of what she's having!' As we continued talking, I realised that Gary was now moving from side to side with a big grin on his face! I asked him to stop and he said, 'No, I'm doing it on purpose!'

With big orange spiders and new stage shirts, off they went for another show, leaving us time to get ready before taking a cab down to the SECC (Scottish Exhibition and Conference Centre).

When the show started, everyone had their spiders on stage with them and Chris and Bernie had dared to wear the shirts we had got for them. We couldn't have been happier because we felt so much a part of this tour now and we were in such a wonderful bubble, away from the trials and tribulations of real life. The show was fantastic and, just before it ended, we ran out of the SECC into a cab and once more beat Gary back to the hotel, making it 3–0 to us, much to his bemusement.

After a quick freshen-up, we piled into the bar and took up the same table as the night before. When Gary joined us, he was with Mikey from Boyzone and they went and sat at a table together. Once again, this highlights the hit-and-miss nature of being on the tour; sometimes your luck is in and sometimes it's not, but you always have to try to make it fun along the way. Despite not speaking to Gary that night, we did have some fun chatting to the band and, when they said they had recorded the concert that evening, we went up to their room to have a listen and they told us all the funny backstage jokes that were going on at the time and how when they were rehearsing they had made some of the lyrics much ruder to have a laugh and that Gary would have to try to remember not to sing them during the actual concert! At one point, we thought we heard a knock at the door and I looked out of the spyhole and told them that Gary was there. They looked a little concerned and so we offered to hide in the bathroom, but then of course, when they opened the door, no one was there because I had just been winding them up!

The next morning, it was time to pack up again and this time we headed off to Manchester, to yet another Malmaison. We knew there was a good chance that Gary wouldn't stay, as his mansion (which he still shared with fiancée Dawn) was close enough to drive back to, but the band would be there and so we decided to stay anyway. The concert at the Manchester Nynex that evening was fantastic – everyone was in high spirits and we spotted Howard in the audience, along with Gary's brother Ian, sister-in-law Lisa and their baby son Lewis. When Gary sang 'War Is Over', lots of glitter fell from the ceiling; it was really beautiful and the band kept smiling at us and laughing at the bits of the show they had told us about the previous night. As predicted, Gary did not stay at the Malmaison, but we had fun with the band nonetheless until the early hours.

The next day, with no concert to rush to, I enjoyed a meal in the Malmaison restaurant and then Tracy drove us to her flat in Cheltenham, where we caught up on sleep.

The following afternoon, we made the short journey to the

Birmingham NEC for the sixth show of the tour, marking the halfway point. So many people had refunded their tickets at the NEC that they had actually pulled a curtain around about halfway back so the place didn't look so empty! That was a really horrible feeling and I wondered how Gary must have felt that night too. Once again, we doubted that he would stay in the Hyatt hotel with the rest of the band, but we stayed there anyway.

The band sat at one table and us girls at another, though they did highly recommend the hotel's Long Island iced teas to us, which were indeed rather lovely. Despite Gary's absence, there was one famous face in the bar that night – Huey from the Fun Lovin' Criminals. Towards the end of the evening, I had run out of cigarettes and was having a wander to see if I could borrow one from someone when Huey's security guard offered me one. I asked him if he thought Huey would mind if I spoke to him and asked for a photo. He said that it would be fine, although I should move fast because he looked as though he was about to go to bed.

I walked over and put my hand on Huey's arm while saying his name and he turned towards me. 'I've just been chatting with your security and he said it was OK to come and speak to you and maybe get a picture,' I said.

Huey was very laidback, and we walked off together away from the bar area and Tracy took some photos of us. I told him how much I loved the Barry White song they did, especially since my mum had told me that I was, in fact, a Barry White baby and he elbowed me knowingly. I apologised for disturbing him, but he said it was fine because he liked to hug and then gave me an unexpected, but very nice cuddle. He asked why I was in Birmingham, and, not wanting to admit the awful truth, I told him that I was one of Gary Barlow's backing singers and that we had played the Birmingham NEC that night. Thankfully, he didn't ask me to try to sing! He said he had played at the Birmingham NIA that night, and, after another hug, we said goodnight and then I went off to bed.

The next day we drove up to Sheffield Arena: front-row seats for concert number seven. The band still had their

With Huey from the Fun Lovin' Criminals, Birmingham, December 1999.

spiders on the stage and we smiled and laughed with them during the show. We decided not to stay in the hotel that night as Gary was once again driving home afterwards, and the following day, with no show and no hotel, we just relaxed at my flat in Brighton.

The next concert was Wembley Arena, where Gary had put in some extras to make it special – for example, at the end during 'War Is Over', a children's choir joined him on stage and once again glittery bits of paper came falling down from the ceiling. He had some of his old band mates there, including Mark Owen, and also a few celebrity pals like Robson Green. Dawn was there too, and during 'Relight My Fire' she was dancing with a pal in the audience the way she had on Take That's final tour in 1995. After the show, they all headed backstage for an aftershow party.

The next day I didn't have far to travel as the tour moved down to Brighton. In the morning I had my hair styled in an up do at Toni & Guy and then Tracy and I went shopping to buy Gary and the band some jokey Christmas presents that we planned to give to them later at the hotel. As it was my home gig, I dressed up really nice and then we checked into the Thistle hotel, wrapped up the presents and then waited in the lobby, where we saw the band arrive in the afternoon. Lorraine made the journey with her fiancé Jason and we had some drinks in the bar before we left.

I was fairly tipsy by the time we got to the concert and went to our front-row seats, but we had a lot of fun. Gary pulled a few faces at us during the show – I think he realised we were a bit merry as we danced and sang along with him! After the show we returned to the hotel; Lorraine told me that Gary had arrived back already and so we went to get the Christmas presents and then got a table in the bar. Gary and the band came to sit at the table next to us with his manager, Kristina. On various trips to the bar, we chatted to the band and ordered more and more drinks.

On the way back from one refuelling trip, I touched Gary's arm and said, 'All right, love?' and he gestured for me to bend down and kiss his cheek. There were no seats free and so I crouched down as he asked me if I had been drunk at the concert – it had looked that way from the stage! I told him that I might have had a few, but that I lived there so it was a special show. He said he remembered that I lived in Brighton and I explained that I only lived up the road so it was pretty crazy to be staying in the hotel! He said that I looked very nice that evening and then he told me that he didn't really like the hotel and would have preferred to stay at The Grand, a little further along the road.

Gary told me that Howard was there but that he had assumed he was at The Grand and had gone there, wandering around asking for him, and we were both laughing. When Howard joined us, Gary introduced him to me as 'Paul' for some reason, but I played along and said, 'Nice to meet you, Paul.' I had never really spent time with Howard before, but he was hilarious and really good fun.

The girls had warned me not to get the presents out in front of Gary's manager as they were quite rude (mainly having come from Ann Summers) but, as I was so drunk by this point, I decided that now was the time and I proceeded to hand them all out, much to the amusement of the band. One of the presents we had bought was a small vibrator (thanks to a comment Gary had made about the light sabre I bought him) and Howard kept switching it on and spinning it round the table and laughing. I continued to chat to Gary and we talked about his relationship with Robbie. I said that he should give Robbie another chance as he seemed like such a hurt person; having played at Slane Castle that year to a crowd of more than 80,000, Robbie had said afterwards that he *still* didn't feel happiness, but Gary said that he was sick of having Robbie throw his friendship back in his face and was tired of giving him chances.

We talked again about his second album and his music in general and how he had delayed releasing his new material for so long. I told him that perhaps the public had seen that long gap and the two postponements of his tour as a sign of defeat in the face of Robbie's success. I also told him that a lot of his songs seemed a bit too nice and that sometimes better songs come from experiencing some pain in your life and in that sense struggles can be very productive for a creative person.

We discussed the arrangement for 'Lie To Me' at the Boardwalk in Sheffield and how he had given extra drama to the mid-section, making it a bit Shirley Bassey, whereas I told him that I thought the song was big enough without that, something that in hindsight he agreed with. I balanced the mild criticism by telling him how great his voice was live and how attractive he was when he played the piano, where you could see he was really feeling the music. He blushed and told me that I was embarrassing him, though, so I apologised and said that hadn't been my intention. Continuing on the musical theme, I told him that I couldn't remember the name of the artist he had recommended to me back in Glasgow, so, knowing that I probably would forget again, he took a napkin and a pen and wrote the name down for me this time. Yes, I still have that napkin and two great albums by the artist recommended, Kirk Franklin!

I said that I had seen Mark at Wembley and asked how he was, and that I had seen Dawn there too and it looked as though she was growing her hair out. I asked if she was growing it for their upcoming wedding and he said, 'Yeah, and she looks like fucking Ken Dodd in the morning!'

As I chatted to Gary, my friends kindly kept bringing me drinks; even Claudia from Portugal was there that night and she said to me later that she couldn't believe how I had chatted to Gary for so long. Eventually, though, after a wonderful evening, Gary said that he needed to go to bed and, soon after, Howard left too, clutching many of the naughty gifts in his arms as he left! He gave me a kiss goodnight, which was very sweet considering I had only just met him really, and I told him to have fun with his goodies!

Another morning, another hangover and also today a panic about what I had said to Gary the previous night. Did I really tell him he needed more misery in his life to be a better songwriter? I knew there must have been huge chunks of conversation that I couldn't even remember, given the length of time we chatted versus what I could recall. I was really worried about seeing him again in light of what had been said and might have been said. The girls couldn't even reassure me as they had not been close enough to hear our conversation but they did say that Gary had looked relaxed and happy throughout and would just have walked away if there had been a problem.

After packing up and having breakfast, I sat in the lobby area chatting to Claudia and then out walked Gary from the lift and my heart pounded as he made his way over to me. He complained that he had a cold sore and in my anxiety I told him that he wanted to watch where he put his mouth! Thankfully, he laughed and then told me that he had got it from a microphone. He asked me if I had seen any of the band and so I directed him to where they were gathered, waiting to leave. Tracy had ordered us a cab back to my flat where I had left my car and it turned up just as Gary was leaving. We went through the revolving doors and I gave him some sweets that I had taken from the reception counter. Just before he got on to the tour bus, he looked at me and said, 'I'll see *you* later,' and I felt sure I was going to get a telling-off for the night before!

After retrieving my car, we drove to Bournemouth to check into the Dormy hotel there and I felt sad, knowing this was the final night with Gary as he had already told us that he was not going to stay after the last show. We went to the restaurant area (which was in a separate building) to get something to eat, only to find Gary sitting there, enjoying some food with the band. We hadn't known that he was going to be in there and I didn't want him to think that we followed him, and so I decided to leave and Eileen came with me.

We were walking the short dark path back to the main building of the hotel when we heard someone running behind us and then I was grabbed from behind. I screamed and then started laughing as I realised that it was Gary who now had an arm round both of us and was growling like a tiger. He asked me how I was feeling and I groaned but said that I would be up for another drinking session later. Eileen asked him if he was going to be drinking that night and he said yes, as it was the last night before he went home.

After he had gone off to his room, we also went to get ready. I called my old friend JoJo in Coventry and told her everything that had been happening and she couldn't believe how well I was getting on with Gary now, compared to the early days when just seeing them walk past us seemed enough. Now he was running after me and putting his arm around me; it was a lot to take in. I got ready for the penultimate concert and we took a taxi down to the Bournemouth International Centre. There were plenty of smiles and acknowledgements between our group, Gary and the band that night during the show. One highlight of the evening was Gary keeping the promise he made in Glasgow and showing me that he was wearing his R2D2 socks – 'beaudy', as Gary would say! Despite this, it was still a horrible feeling to know that it was all coming to an end.

Back at the hotel, we noticed that a couple of pool tables had been reserved in the games room and so we decided to get some drinks and wait in there, securing the only other available table in the room. Also, it would look better to be in there already than to follow Gary in after he had entered. The risk paid off, and soon members of the band started arriving, and everyone was in the mood to party because it was the last night we would all be in a hotel together.

When Gary came in, he said hello and went to play pool on the table by the door. The pseudonym he had used on this tour was 'Dick Grayson', and while out shopping one day we had seen a great Christmas card that read, 'Everyone loves Dick at Christmas' with an old-fashioned picture of a young chap supposedly named Richard on the front. We thought, given Gary's chosen fake name, this would be a perfect card to give to him from all of us, thanking him for a great tour and wishing him a Merry Christmas.

We waited until he came over to us to give him the card and, when he opened it, he really loved it and thought it was very funny. I then told him I was sorry about last night and asked him if I had said anything too horrible or stupid, but he surprised me by replying, 'No, not at all, it was all beautiful, don't you worry.' He then proceeded to tell us another really dirty joke that we didn't even really get, not that I can remember it now, but we were taken aback by how sick it was, even by Gary's standards. But he just loved to shock us or make us laugh. He went back over to his game of pool and I think he found it quite odd as we partied with his band members; he kept looking over as if he wanted to join in and we didn't know whether to invite him over or leave him be.

During the evening, we took lots of photos to remember the tour, lots of us with the band, and, when we all gathered for a group shot, Gary again looked over; I wished I had just said to him to come and be in it too, it would have been perfect. After a few more games of pool, Gary decided to call it a night and he came over to say goodbye. Soon after, he made a telephone call down to Chris to ask for a joint to smoke as he was having some trouble sleeping. Chris said that he had done this a few times and it explained why, earlier in Brighton, Gary had asked me if I had tried any of Chris's weed during the tour and commented on how good it was.

With Gary gone, it was up to us to carry on the party into the early hours again – even poor old Bernie (who was usually to be found sipping tea in the corner) was drunk and asked me to help him find his room! It had been such an amazing two weeks and we had become close to all of the people we had travelled together with over this time. All the drunken nights, the fun, the laughter and just the feeling of being part of something like that, but now it was all ending and, with Gary's career in tatters, we knew deep down that this would never happen again.

The next day, the band gathered by the real log fire in the reception area and we sat with them as they waited to leave. As always, everyone was hungover and tired, but also feeling sad that that night would be the final show. Gary soon joined us, wearing a big grey coat that looked like a duvet and seemed to be keeping him very warm. We stood at the front of the hotel, and, with tears in my eyes, I asked him for a big hug, just one last time, and we cuddled for ages – I just didn't want to let go. He asked me where my car was, and then told me to follow the tour bus to Cardiff to make sure we got there OK, and so as they loaded into their bus we got into our cars and then off we went in a little convoy.

About halfway into the journey, Gary's bus pulled into a petrol station and we pulled up behind. He went inside the shop and looked at some snacks with Tracy, Eileen and Lucy, but I stayed in my car. Chris came to have a look at it and then he offered to show me inside the tour bus. All through the tour we had made jokes about it as it seemed so small compared to the big tour coaches you normally see, and so he wanted to show that it wasn't that bad inside, which indeed it wasn't. I went back to my car and Gary smiled and waved as he walked past to get back into the bus.

When we arrived at Cardiff International Arena, we pulled over and watched as he left the bus and spent time signing autographs and having his photo taken with some fans that had waited there to see him.

A couple of hours later, we were inside the venue, waiting for the very last show. We chatted to some of the band as they walked around by the merchandising section and then we went to watch the support act, Nicole Lacy. She began her set by saying how sad she felt that it was the end of the tour and how some people in the crowd tonight had been with the tour the whole way and so we gave a loud cheer in recognition. When she sang Madonna's song 'Take A Bow', we were all nearly in tears. Once Gary came out on to the stage, I tried to hang on to every moment, knowing that soon it would all be in the past. Every song he sang held so many memories and every smile meant so much.

When he began to sing 'War Is Over' for the final time, we held up banners that said, 'Tour Is Over!' The band saw them first and were laughing, and then, when Gary spotted them, he winked and then sang the lyrics, 'Tour is over' and gave us a smile.

Soon the show had ended and it was time to go home. I could never have imagined what a great time I would have on that tour and how sad it would feel for it to end.

13

MOVING ON

As predicted, the end of Gary's second solo tour also marked the end of his once hugely successful solo career, and, unless you count an appearance on the ITV drama *Heartbeat*, there really wasn't anything left for us to go to see him. We kept up our friendship with drummer Chris Dagley and would meet up at the Boaters in Kingston, Surrey, to watch him play live jazz. Gary married his long-term girlfriend Dawn in January 2000, and the following month Chris revealed to us that she was expecting their first child.

Eileen and I went up to Newcastle on 19 February to see Robbie perform there and stayed once more at the Newcastle Malmaison, so full of memories, although Robbie was elsewhere and so we didn't see him.

In the spring of that year, Mark was out promoting his upcoming TV series, *Mark's Celebrity Vespas*, in which he and some famous pals, such as Ralf Little, would travel around the

Euro 2000 football match venues in Belgium on scooters. One morning we went to the ITV studios to see him arrive for *This Morning* and we chatted to him for a while. Radiohead were going to be playing soon in London and I asked him if he was going, but he said that he didn't have any tickets. 'I thought you would be able to get on the guest list,' I commented, and he told me that he wished that were true!

Having never met any of the lads at their homes (bar a few encounters with Robbie and the sunny afternoon with Jason), I was persuaded one day to make the drive all the way up to Leck in the Lake District to see if we could see Mark. We didn't know exactly the location of his house and, as we pulled over to the side of the road and got out to look at one property, Lucy (the Mark expert) told me that he was driving our way in his Land Rover. As he passed, I smiled and waved, and he smiled and waved back. We drove in the direction he had come from and soon found his house and parked up nearby. Lucy reassured me that she had heard that Mark was always very lovely to people at his house and I needn't worry.

When he returned home, he delayed going into his gates and pulled over and got out of his vehicle to talk to us. He said that he had just been playing football. I said that we had seen him drive past and that was us waving earlier and asked if he hadn't noticed those two mad fans at the roadside, but he said, 'No, I thought you were just happy people!'

We had some photos taken with him and asked if many fans came up to his house and he said that a few still did.

I left Lucy to chat to him some more, as she knew him much

Mark with Lucy at his house in Leck.

better than I did, and then we thanked Mark for his time and started the long journey home. As I waited to turn right into a petrol station about ten minutes later, a car came smashing into the back of me, giving us both quite a shock. Not sure as to the extent of the damage, we decided that we would need to be towed home and it took three AA vans to do the journey all the way from the Lake District to Brighton!

After that, it really was time to move on, with six years spent in the quest to meet Take That with some pretty impressive results, especially where Gary was concerned, but now I had to accept their absence from my life. Having not worked for the past few years, I knew I had to stop spending my winnings or very soon the whole Lottery fund would have been exhausted! The first thing I did was to get a job in the call centre of Cable and Wireless (later NTL, or, as we referred to it, 'Empty Hell'). There I met some new friends and began socialising in ways that didn't involve ex-members of Take That or hotel bars and lobbies!

I quickly realised that I had never had a 'real' friendship with Gary; I mean he knew that I was in contact with Chris Dagley

Me with Mark at Leck.

but he never once passed a message through him to say hello to me. Although I would always take an interest in what happened to the five guys that used to be Take That (I had a 'Google alert' set up for each of them on my computer so that I would receive the latest news), they were in my conscious mind less and less as I got on with my life. By now, only Robbie was out there, making a huge success of his career, but I just didn't have the will to even attempt to try to see him while he was playing sell-out shows at Knebworth – he had become even more massive than Take That themselves!

Just over five years after my extended goodbye hug to Gary at the Dormy hotel in Bournemouth, I received some information (via the Google alert) about an event I thought he might attend and discussed with Lorraine the possibility that we might go – 'for old times' sake' and because it coincided with my 29th birthday!

Despite no longer releasing records, Gary had kept himself busy by writing for other artists such as Delta Goodrem, Blue and Charlotte Church, not to mention becoming a father twice over, with the birth of his son Daniel in 2000 and daughter Emily in 2002.

In 2005, he had also written a song for a musical called *Love Shack* that was due to open soon in Manchester, starring Faye Tozer from Steps. I had a feeling that he would attend the press opening night that I had heard about and Lorraine and I decided that we would go along and then celebrate my birthday in Manchester afterwards. We didn't know for sure if he was going to be there but we managed to convince Eileen to come along too.

It was such a strange feeling to be packing and travelling up the motorway for another Gary jaunt. Would we see him? Would it still be the same? Five years was a really long time and we all had moved on in our lives. When we arrived at the theatre, there were some paparazzi outside, but they wouldn't tell me who they were there for. Within a few minutes, the cameras began flashing and in walked Gary. He looked so different with his hair quite long and he had put on quite a bit of weight since we had last seen him. I walked over to where he stood and he seemed surprised to see me. He remarked, 'Oh, haven't we aged!' and I said, 'Thank you for that!'

As there were cameras and people around, I asked if it was OK to hug him as it had been so long and he said of course it was, and so I gave him a big hug. I told him that it was my birthday so he wished me a happy one and then Dawn came over to join us. I smiled at her, but she didn't look at me and then they went off to enjoy the performance.

Gary was only sitting a few rows behind us but was not even being disturbed; we tried to find him in the interval but to no avail and resorted to trying to see him as he left, which again we missed. As we walked along the road to try to get a cab, we saw a silver Porsche Jeep emerge from an NCP and Eileen said, 'I bet that's Gary.' Sure enough, it was indeed him driving himself to the aftershow party. We went to the Malmaison for a few birthday drinks and, although we didn't see Gary, we did have some fun with Sam and Mark from the *Pop Idol* competition. They were there filming for the Saturday-morning TV show they presented with Fearne Cotton and they even bought me a birthday drink.

In 2004, rumours had started about there being a possible Take That reunion. Apparently, during a 19 Management party, Gary had been overheard discussing it; however, Chris Dagley (who was still in contact with Gary) told us that he had been at Gary's new home in Kensington recently and had been told that it wasn't true. It wasn't long before the rumours started again and in 2005 they gained credence when Take That announced a press conference at the end of November. After ten years apart, were they really planning to announce a reunion tour? We waited and we hoped.

14

THE ULTIMATE REUNION

Gary began the November 2005 press conference in exactly the same way as the February 1996 one, with the words, 'Unfortunately, the rumours are true' – except that this time he wasn't bringing us bad news but thanking everyone for giving them the last ten years off and revealing an 11-date arena tour for the following year.

The Take That reunion inspired a mini reunion between me and my old Take That friends as we began to call each other to find out which concerts we were planning to go to and who was going to try to get tickets for which venue. At the time, I was studying for my psychology degree and had fallen in love with and got engaged to a wonderful guy called Ben, who I had met while studying. He didn't mind me rekindling my lost love for Take That, but I only planned to go to one or two concerts on the new tour.

When the tickets went on sale, I was fully prepared for the

fight to come, especially these days with the Internet and eBay, where a £40 ticket in a good position can sell for hundreds of pounds. I had two computer screens and a telephone, and at 9 a.m. I tried to get the tickets for whatever shows I could. Such was the level of demand that the Ticketmaster website crashed almost straight away and the phone lines were permanently engaged. None of us – not me, Lorraine, Eileen, Lucy, Tracy or Debbie – could get a ticket that day. The only people that we knew had done it were those who had queued at the actual venues overnight. Despite a 10-year absence, the demand for tickets was phenomenal!

The band revealed in radio interviews later that day that they genuinely hadn't expected – after all these years – that tickets would sell out so fast and that they were astonished at the response from their loyal fans. Despite their later announcing more shows, even at Wembley Stadium, I never got a ticket. I decided that I would go up to Newcastle anyway for the beginning of the tour and try to somehow get my hands on a ticket. There was no way I could miss the moment when Take That walked back on to the stage again; I *had* to hear the roar from the crowd and see their faces as they were welcomed back. I resorted to the dreaded eBay and got some tickets about halfway back, costing £50 each, and then excitedly I drove up to Newcastle with Lorraine for the first show of the reunion tour.

We decided to go a day early, which is when the band normally arrived in preparation for the concert the next day. Everyone met at the Newcastle Malmaison and it seemed as if we had never been away! We began calling all the hotels in the area for 'Paul Turner' or 'Chris Healey' and we tracked them down to the Hilton hotel across the water. As the others were still getting ready, Lorraine and I walked over to the Hilton to keep a watch for arrivals and were not disappointed when, soon after taking our seats in the foyer, a huge tour bus pulled up at the front of the hotel.

I was on the phone to Eileen, giving her the latest, when I saw my old pal Bernie get off the coach. I walked over to him and we said hello. I asked him how he was and if they were excited about the show tomorrow and if Gary and the others were staying at this hotel too. He said that he honestly didn't know but that they had left at the same time so, if they were staying here, then they would be arriving any minute. The other girls came rushing over from the Malmaison and we had a few drinks in the lobby, but, as time passed, it became clear that Take That were not staying in this hotel.

I went to the bar and asked guitarist Milton what the show was like and what songs the lads were going to perform, but he said he couldn't tell me and that I would have to wait until the next day! Then Bernie came over and we chatted, and he kindly bought me a drink. The night wore on and in the end we gave up, and walked back to the Malmaison and went to bed.

The next day, the search was on again for Take That's hotel. Lorraine and I had popped into town as I wanted to get some new shoes and we received a call from the others to say that they had found the lads! One local newspaper printed a picture of Take That arriving at their hotel the previous evening and the girls had shown this picture to a local cab driver, who had recognised the type of cobbled ground and stone plant pot and identified it as the Marriott hotel, Gosforth Park. We were warned that hotel staff there were now asking whether or not you were a resident when you showed up at the hotel, so it was with some nerves that we tried to make our way into the back entrance and towards reception.

The manager did indeed ask us a few questions but we claimed that we were just there to meet somebody and asked why he was asking us questions; he told us that Take That were at the hotel and that one of them was in the bar at that very moment. We thought this was pretty indiscreet, but I think he was just so excited himself about having the guys there. The 'one of them' was Gary and I had a quick peek and then all the anxiety began again. Despite already having non-refundable rooms at the Malmaison hotel, we all now booked rooms at the Marriott for that evening and then sat in the bar area and ordered some drinks.

Gary had moved into the restaurant for some lunch and I was really nervous about seeing him again. After an hour or so, I saw from the corner of my eye that he was about to walk through with Dawn (who was dancing on the tour) and then the next thing I knew he was standing beside me and was bending down to kiss my cheek! It had been such a long time and I was quite flustered, so I said, 'Oh, you can't just kiss *me*, Gary, what about the others?'

He leaned towards Eileen to kiss her cheek too but then left it at that. I told him that we had seen Bernie and Milton the

Gary with me and Lorraine, Marriott hotel, April 2006.

night before and that they had refused to give us any details about the concert and Gary replied, 'Well, you'll find out tonight, won't you!' I asked if he was nervous but he said that he was doing OK.

Someone who was very nervous was Jason, who was really suffering from anticipated stage fright. We asked him if he was OK and he told us how bad he felt, but we reassured him that he could get up on stage and sing 'Baa Baa Black Sheep' and still get a huge cheer! Howard walked around with his girlfriend and baby daughter Lola, who was a real cutie, and then Mark came down with his pregnant girlfriend, Emma. Things were certainly very different now from the old days; instead of picking out girls to sleep with and having wild drunken nights, they (except Jason) were accompanied by their 'WAGs' and things would ultimately be very different the second time around. Over the years there had been many rumours flying around about who Jason may or may not have dated, including TV presenters Jenny Powell and Paula Yates and even Lulu who had joined the band several times on

The band about to set off for the first show of their 2006 reunion tour.

stage to sing their hit 'Relight My Fire'. Howard seemed to confirm the relationship in a 2005 interview with Jonathan Ross when he famously stated, after being asked by Jonathan if he had slept with Lulu, that it was in fact Jason who had slept with her!

After everyone had got on to the tour bus and left for the Newcastle Metro Arena, we went back to our original hotel to get ready and pack up to move to our second hotel! Once at the arena, it was like stepping back in time: girls were wearing old tour T-shirts and some had even drawn Take That signs on their faces, whistles were being blown and already there was an amazing atmosphere. As show time got nearer and nearer, the excitement was building and inside the arena I was almost in tears as I saw the familiar 'waiting for Take That' routines of Mexican waves, screams and foot-stamping that brought back so many memories from the first time.

The moment those four guys came back out on to that stage was everything I had imagined and more; it was worth every penny and effort it had taken to be there! My hair stood on end, the screaming and cheering was so intense that it was just like welcoming a long-lost relative back into your life that you hadn't seen for years but were so thrilled to meet again. They just stood there smiling, their eyes filling up; the emotion was incredible, reconnecting to something very special that had happened a long time ago and bringing it right up to date. Then they began to play and every single minute they were on that stage it just kept getting better and better. Rearranging 'It Only Takes A Minute' into a sexy tango was a stroke of genius: who would have known such a cheesy song could sound that good?

The energy, the dancing, even break-dancing, and in the middle a hologram appeared of Robbie singing 'Could It Be Magic' that he had specially recorded for the show. Yet again they had outdone themselves, and, just when you thought they couldn't do any more, rain started to pour down on to the stage and they came out to sing 'Back For Good' before removing their jackets and splashing around in tight wet T-shirts! It was, and I think always will be, the most amazing concert I have ever been to.

When it was all over, we were buzzing and couldn't believe how good it had all been and we made a dash back to the Marriott hotel. While waiting for Take That to return, we talked about old times and things we had done to meet them. There weren't many fans at the hotel; probably because it was about twelve miles out of town, we seemed to be the only ones, although we did make quite a big group. I had an idea that when the guys returned we should stand up and give them a round of applause. As it was so late, I worried that they would come in and go straight to bed and I wanted to get their attention.

When the tour bus finally pulled up at the front, we all agreed to go ahead and do it, and, as Jason walked in, we treated him to the first round of applause. He smiled at us and waved, and then we did the same for Howard and Mark, who also found it funny that we were doing that. Finally, Gary came in with Dawn and, while she went off upstairs, he came over to speak to us. 'What did you think then?' he asked, rubbing his hands together. We all told him how fantastic we thought the show was and then a rather drunk Debbie said, 'Yeah, so fuck you, Robbie!' Gary looked surprised and then smiled.

Just as he was walking away, I decided to go after him and I said, 'Gary, sorry, I know you're tired, but this is the only show I am planning to do on this tour so I wondered if I could have a photo now?'

He replied, shocked, 'What, only one show? What's the matter with you?'

I explained that I was now engaged and that life moves on, showing him the jewelled fourth finger of my left hand. 'Life certainly does move on,' he said, and he then put his arm around me for the photo. As he pulled me in close, he wished me every happiness for the future and I could tell that he really meant it. There was so much I wanted to say, to thank him for all his kindness and all the happiness he had brought into my life, but I couldn't say anything and, before I knew it, the others had got up to ask for photos and were all busy posing with him and then he was gone again. It's probably not very important to Gary, but I would have liked the opportunity to really thank him and to apologise for my misdemeanours! (If you're reading this, Mr Barlow, then job done!)

We carried on drinking, and then, about half an hour later, Mark came down to the bar to smoke a cigarette. On his way back to his room, he asked us if we had all enjoyed the concert and if we were coming to any more shows on the tour.

By about 3 a.m., I knew that I had to get to bed as my older self would not be able to handle the hangover as well as I used to! The next morning we returned to the Malmaison for breakfast (which had been included in our room rate) and then we set off home.

I hadn't planned to do any more shows on the tour, but then one day Eileen called and asked me if I wanted to buy two of her Wembley tickets as she had just bought some better fifth-row ones. I took her up on the offer and decided to treat my fiancé to the Take That experience. Oddly enough, he loved the show – it couldn't have been anything to do with the scantily clad dancers, could it?

We knew that the Conrad was as always the hotel of choice for the London shows but we were so stuck in traffic that we didn't get there until after midnight. I walked in by myself as security is tight there and a whole group of girls would have aroused suspicion. I saw James and Paul, the same security guys they have always had, standing by the door to the bar and I walked inside. Gary was on a stool at the bar, facing outwards towards the room, and as I passed I said hello, but that I was looking for the toilet.

When I returned to the bar I managed to order a glass of wine but, when my friends came in, the bar was closed and then Eileen told me that my fiancé had been questioned by security and wasn't happy. I went over to Gary and said that I was going, but that I had seen the show again and it was absolutely amazing, and he replied with a big warm smile, 'What did you expect, it *is* us!' I totally got his point and I kissed his cheek before leaving the bar. It had been a brief visit, but Mark had been in the bar too and it had been nice to say hello.

A few days later, my friends (who had returned to the Conrad) called me excitedly to reveal that Robbie Williams had been in the hotel. I was really jealous not to witness that reunion; they reported that Gary and Robbie had even hugged each other and said that they would see each other soon! If only I had been there; I would have loved to have seen that. As it turned out, due to my studies and my relationship, I didn't go to any more concerts on that tour and was merrily getting on with my life, but things don't always turn out as you plan and my life was to change again so much that by their next tour I would be free to take part, just like the old days.

15

'BEAUTIFUL WORLD' TOUR: EUROPE

When tickets for the 'Beautiful World' tour went on sale, I was still settled in my relationship and studying hard at university, and so I did not enter into the fight to get my hands on any tickets at the point of release. Having been unsuccessful last time anyway, I thought, if I decided that I did want to go to any shows nearer the time, I could always try to get last-minute ones. As the tour was beginning in October 2007, though, my beautiful world changed when my relationship ended and I thought what better remedy than to drift away into my unreality again and spend some time on the lads' tour and having fun with the girls? I was already hearing reports back from friends who had gone to some of the shows in Europe and so I decided to just pack up a bag (or several) and go!

With my fear of flying now at phobia level, I decided to drive over to France via the Eurotunnel and then continue to

Hamburg with my car for their show on 31 October. I was going to try for last-minute tickets at the box office and then see if I could find their hotel. I went with a good friend – not a Take That fan but someone who knew that I needed to get away! The day before the show, we drove around Hamburg, looking at the likely hotels there to see if there were any signs (groups of girls standing outside, for example), but there was nothing.

The next day I headed to the Color Line Arena and waited for Take That to arrive. I saw the familiar face of Chris Healey chatting to some of the dancers and then we overheard his

The Color Line Arena in Hamburg.

discussion with a photographer about when and where Take That would be arriving, so we waited nearby along with about another twenty girls. As concert venues in Europe offered standing tickets, most of the other girls were in a queue around the corner to make a mad dash to the front row! The guys finally arrived at about 5.30 p.m. to the usual array of camera flashes and shouting from the assembled crowd. I made a note of the vehicles they were using (silver VW vans with blacked-out windows) and took details of the number plates as we still didn't know the hotel we were going to have to follow them to from the Arena after the show.

After posing for photos, Gary, Mark, Jason and Howard went inside the building. Days before travelling to Hamburg, it was on the news that Howard had sustained a serious injury while performing on stage and he was now in hospital with a collapsed lung. He had had to miss some of the shows and we were worried the tour would be cancelled, but the other three carried on without him. During the last show a message that Howard had recorded from his hospital bed had been played on the screen, but to see him arriving this evening was a good sign.

We walked around to the box office but it was still closed and so we decided to take a walk around the arena to keep warm. My friend asked me, 'Isn't that Mark Owen?' and I looked just by the door where they had arrived about half an hour earlier and there he was, having a cigarette, completely undisturbed by the girls who had all moved round to the other side of the building. Mark was joined by Take That's new manager, Jonathan Wild, and, although my stomach flipped over with nerves, I decided to be brave and walk over to them. 'Hi, Mark, my name is Claire. I was wondering if you could do me a favour?' Mark smiled and said hello, before I continued, 'Could you please pass a message on to Gary for me and tell him that Lottery Girl is here. You see, I don't have any tickets tonight and I wondered if he could help.' I explained to Mark that I wasn't crazy, and that it was Gary who had given me that name after I won some money on the Lottery. He asked me for my real name again and then I told him I would wait in the same area and suggested that Chris Healey could come out to meet me there. Mark said he would do that and I thanked him and walked back towards my friend, shaking with nerves!

It wasn't more than five minutes before Chris Healey came out from the building, calling my name, and I walked towards him and then shook his hand and kissed his cheek. I didn't want to come across too cheeky so I said that I didn't mind going to the box office to get tickets, but I just thought that I would ask. He said that it wasn't a problem and that he would go and get me a couple of guest wristbands in a minute. I asked him if Howard was feeling better and he said that it might be a few more shows before he was back on stage. I told him that Howard should come on stage tonight just to say hello to the crowd and Chris smiled and said that they were going to do that, but it was a surprise!

I admitted that I had never been to see Take That in Europe before and then we talked about the 'Ultimate' tour and how they had not known what to expect from the first night in

Newcastle and were completely blown away by the response from the crowd. I said that they *must* have known they would get that kind of reaction but I suppose they see it from a different point of view to their fans. After Chris had gone and got the wristbands for us, I thanked him wholeheartedly and practically skipped off, feeling very lucky and excited about seeing the show.

Chris had advised us that the best position inside was close to the B stage on the side nearest to the main stage and, when we went inside, this was exactly where we went and we ended up right at the front of the B stage. We watched the support act, Jamie Scott and the Town, and had a few drinks; I chatted to a German lady who couldn't believe I had come all the way from the UK to see Take That and she was making such a big fuss that I ended up showing her my wristband arm and saying, 'Well, actually I am with the band!'

Just before the show started, a message was played to say that Howard would not be joining the rest of the band on stage that evening and that refunds were available up until 8.40 p.m. Then the lights went down, there was a huge scream and the show began. I had watched many clips of the tour on YouTube so I knew what to expect but it was still amazing to see it live. The lapdancing that accompanies 'It Only Takes A Minute' was by far the raunchiest thing they had done yet and mixing Gnarls Barkley's massive hit 'Crazy' in with 'Relight My Fire' was another masterstroke that the crowd adored.

When Howard came out on to the stage, he did so in a hospital gown that was open at the back and on the screens by the side of the stage you could see that he was naked underneath. The crowd were screaming and laughing as he kept flashing his bum! I don't know if the other three had known that he planned to come on stage like that, but they seemed genuinely surprised, and Gary was laughing so much he was nearly crying! Howard then read a message in German, explaining how frustrating it was not to be able to perform with the others, who he thanked for continuing without him before jokingly adding, 'Bastards!' and then exited the stage, flashing more buttocks as he did so.

'I'd Wait For Life' almost had me in tears; when Gary sits at his piano and plays a ballad like that, I can't help but be moved. When they came to the B stage, I felt sure that Gary would see me there in the front, but he just didn't seem to look my way once! After Jason had sung 'Wooden Boat' to an amazing response from the crowd, the arena was transformed into a gigantic rave as dance music pumped out and the boys took us all back to the early Nineties with 'Give Good Feeling' and even added in the bit from the 'Pops' tour, where they get on their knees and crawl slowly towards the audience.

Since we had to make it back to the car to try to follow the VW vans when they left, we walked out of the arena as 'Never Forget' began and almost into Chris Healey, who might well have wondered why on earth we were leaving so early! We sat at the end of the road and waited for the vans to appear. But we made one very silly mistake: we parked by some traffic lights and, when Take That zoomed past, they were of course on red! I think, had it been back in 1995, I would have driven

Mark sitting on the piano during the Hamburg concert.

straight through but I was not willing to compromise anyone's life just to see Take That and following now would be done only at a distance and within speed limits. By the time we set off, we had completely lost them and I felt gutted as I had wanted to see Gary in person to thank him for getting me into the show. I wondered if I should just have asked Chris which hotel they were staying in while we had been chatting. Gary had told me hotel information before, but I felt that would be putting him in an awkward position if he had to say no! For a while, we drove around anyway looking once more at the popular hotels, and then gave up. We didn't have a hotel booked at that point, as we had been on standby in case we found out where Take That were staying, so we found ourselves an Ibis hotel next to the lake that still had a room available and got some sleep.

The next day there was a long drive to Rotterdam ahead, and getting stuck in some traffic on the way in made us panic that we wouldn't make it in time to see the show! When we arrived, we decided to flash the same wristbands – which of course we were still wearing, and I would still be now except it fell off through wear and tear – to one of the people on the door and she let us in straight away. I have no idea whether they were using the same wristbands every night or if the woman just saw a wristband and her brain said 'enter' but nevertheless we were ecstatic to be inside for another show. I had heard that Take That might be going to Amsterdam afterwards, as this is something they had done before, but none of my contacts seemed sure of their plans.

We enjoyed the show: Howard came out once more in the hospital gown, flashing his bum, and we even saw Chris Healey and discussed how loud it was that evening! When Jason talked to the crowd, he mentioned his fear of flying and how he had had to endure the long drive from Hamburg to Rotterdam, something I could completely empathise with! He said that he was determined to beat his fears and those included his fear of singing solo, despite the fact that he sounds really good singing 'Wooden Boat' and always gets a loud cheer.

Once again, we left the arena just as 'Never Forget' started and raced around to the car and found a place to pull up to wait for the band to depart. When they did so, it was with a police escort and, as they sped off, a policeman held us back. When we were finally allowed to move, we were once more frustratingly halted by traffic lights and, although we saw the direction in which the VWs had gone, once the lights had turned green and we managed to drive that way, they had gone again. Although we had managed to see both concerts for free, it was frustrating for me not to be able to find the hotel!

After staying in Rotterdam, we decided to take a day off from trying to find Take That and go and have some fun in Amsterdam as there was no concert that evening and we had no idea where the guys were. The following day, we got up early to do another long drive, this time to Stuttgart. The best and most likely hotel appeared to be Le Méridien and, as we drove past at about 5 p.m., there were girls standing outside, giving us hope that finally we might have found the guys! We parked up and went inside to the reception. Two women had dressed up as nurses and were holding a picture of Howard, taken while he was on stage in the hospital gown and flashing his bum. Signs were good, but I needed a bit more confirmation before I booked a room.

I went to reception and said that I needed to speak to the tour manager about which wristband I should use that night (showing the one that was, of course, still around my wrist) and I explained that I didn't know which fake name he was using and asked if she could help. She talked to another receptionist, who printed out a list of names and room numbers, and she came over to me and asked, 'Is it just one room you need?' I told her just the tour manager, but she said she didn't know who was who from the list. It didn't matter; it was completely clear that Take That were resident and all I had to do now was get my friend to go over and book a room!

Feeling very tired from the drive, we decided to give the show a miss and just spend time getting ready in the room, drinking some wine and, thanks to the hotel's satellite system, we were able to watch some of ITV's *The X Factor*. Once we were down in the bar, we went to sit at a table but we were told that we couldn't sit there as it was reserved for a group at 11 p.m. I asked if it was Take That and he smiled. We took the next table along and I started to get very nervous as I pictured Gary coming over to say hello and us having a chat like we used to. My heart was really pounding – even the wine wasn't taking away the anxiety!

Shortly after 11 p.m., as the bar was filling up with girls fresh back from the concert, Take That's security guys, James and Paul, came into the bar. Paul had to move two girls from the reserved table who were kicking up a fuss but he very sternly told them to go, until they finally did so. Some people began sitting at the table and then in walked Howard, saying hello to some of the many girls that were crowded around as he made his way to his seat.

One girl walked over to him and asked him if the others were going to come down and he joked that he would give them a call and tell them to come to the bar. When she walked away, however, he told a friend that Gary had his wife and kids there, and so he had gone straight up to his room. Mark also had his fiancée and baby Elwood there and was also staying upstairs, while Jason was in his room, watching pay TV!

I sat and had a few drinks, but of course I was upset that I had finally found the lads' hotel and I wouldn't get a chance to see Gary to say thank you for Hamburg, or have a quick chat. Howard stayed up until past 1 a.m. At some point, I overheard him discussing the possibility of another tour in 2009! Just after he left and went to bed, we too went to our room.

The next day I had the most awful hangover and couldn't face going down to reception until I was forced to at noon by check-out time. I clutched a bottle of water and sat in the reception area, watching as bags were being loaded into the VWs. James, Paul and the drivers wandered around and there were quite a few girls standing outside the entrance to the hotel. There wasn't a huge amount of girls, so I had no reason to suspect they would do a sneaky side-exit manoeuvre; however, the VWs parked just up from the entrance suddenly moved off at speed and were gone. Everyone was left confused, but, when the girls from outside all cleared off, we thought they must have seen something and that was why they left.

Slightly bored by all the waiting around, my friend had gone off to the bar to get an orange juice and came back with a printed list of names and room numbers under the group name 'Ultimate Touring Limited' that had been left pinned up behind the bar. The first name was Mr M Anthony, which I thought could be Mark's as his full name is Mark Anthony Patrick Owen and there were some funny ones – Mr STD Queen and Mr B Ruff – we had some fun trying to work out who was who!

As we thought the guys had left, we decided to go up to the fourth floor, where their rooms had been situated to confirm that they had indeed gone and maybe we could start the long drive home. However, just as we were walking along, we became even more confused to see Mark, his son Elwood and fiancée Emma sitting on a sofa near the lift, with security guy James standing by the lift doors. Mark looked at me, but I felt so bad for being there that I didn't manage a smile back – I felt I was in his space and hadn't meant to be because we thought they had just left! We pressed the button to call the lift and waited a few horrible moments until it came and we went back to reception.

I overheard a girl who was talking on her mobile saying that

Howard had left at 10 a.m. that morning to catch the train to Berlin because his collapsed lung meant that he couldn't fly. She sounded as if she knew what had been going on and so I went over to talk to her. I told her that I had just seen Mark upstairs and she said that he was her favourite, and that, as most fans had left the hotel now (having seen the VWs leave), he would hopefully just come through reception. She told me that she had been in Hamburg and that the band had stayed at the East Hotel, which I hadn't even heard of. She revealed that Gary had been drinking in the bar and I wanted to cry! I had come all the way to Europe and missed my chances, and to know that he had been in the bar and only five minutes from our hotel was too cruel! She said she knew Mark very well and that he had given her tickets for one of the shows, and I showed her my wristband and explained that it was Gary that I knew the best. We talked about the times we had met them and swapped gossip, and she told me that she was going to come over to Manchester in December to see them.

She told me that she had known about the East Hotel in Hamburg as that is where Mark had stayed on his solo tour and she went on to tell me a lovely story of how, at some point during the evening, Mark had bought drinks for all thirty of his fans that were in the bar. I thought that was a very nice gesture and it just goes to show that they don't really mind us being there in the hotels with them at all.

We waited around in the hotel for another hour or so and then left to begin the long drive back to Calais. My friends were going to the Denmark concerts and they kept trying to persuade me to go with them but I just couldn't face the flight. Besides, it wasn't long before the UK tour would start and, with all their fake names in hand, I could call ahead and find out all the hotels to avoid all the hassle of trying to find them at the time! You could say that was one good thing to have come from the trip, which, free concerts aside, had turned out to be a bit disappointing.

16

'BEAUTIFUL WORLD' TOUR: UK

O n Friday, 16 November 2007, I set off from Brighton with a car full of bags and a diary full of plans, just as I had done on Gary's second tour in 1999. The first stop was Birmingham, where I had managed to get last-minute tickets in the fairly reasonable block 2 at the NEC arena. I met up with Lorraine at the Malmaison hotel as Take That's hotel was fully booked until Sunday. There was a mad rush to get ready and, by the time we got to the arena, we could already hear the first song playing from outside. We had to pick up the tickets from the box office, and so by the time we made it to our seats Take That were already getting lap dances! Afterwards, Mark apologised that they had come on stage late as a woman's waters had broken and they had waited for the ambulance to come and take her away! Six hours later, the woman gave birth to a healthy little girl and named her Clementine – the title of Mark's second solo single!

Gary and a female dancer, Birmingham NEC, November 2007.

The UK crowd were much louder than Europe and it was nice to see them at a home show again. As Jason performed his solo number, I noticed a very cheeky banner in the front row that read, 'Jason, you can put your wood in my boat'. I thought that was very funny, but I'm not sure if Jason would have seen it, as he always sings that song with his eyes closed and usually says afterwards, 'I will do that with my eyes open one day.'

As usual, we left the show as 'Never Forget' began to try to get into Take That's hotel to avoid them asking questions as we arrived. They were staying at the Hotel du Vin, which is the Malmaison's sister hotel, so I came up with the brainwave of asking at the Malmaison reception if we could drink in the du Vin bar that night past 11 p.m. (which is when non-residents are normally asked to leave). The receptionist called the du Vin and asked if this would be OK, and we were advised to let them know at reception when we arrived, but that it would be fine. My plan had worked!

We arrived at the Hotel du Vin and bought a couple of drinks and then sat on a plush brown leather sofa in the reception. Not very long afterwards, one of the silver VW vans pulled up to the front of the hotel and in walked Mark and Howard. Shortly afterwards, in a separate van, Gary's wife Dawn (who was again dancing on the UK leg of the tour) arrived with their children, Daniel and Emily, and they went upstairs. Over an hour later, Gary finally turned up with Jason, both of them carrying plates of food that they must have brought from the venue. As Gary was about to turn the corner, he caught sight of me on the sofa and whipped his head back round and waved hello.

Soon, he came back with Dawn and they went down to the Cellar Bar. Mark was next to walk through reception, saying hello to some of the girls that were gathered at various points along the way, and then he too went down to the Cellar Bar. We stayed in reception for a while and then, when we needed another drink, we decided to go down to the bar too. Most of the dancers were at the hotel that evening for a bit of a party, even though they (like us) were actually staying at the Malmaison.

The bar was pretty full but we managed to get two stools just next to a 'snug' that had been specially reserved for Take That. We didn't have any trouble getting served once we explained that it had been sorted out earlier and then Mark came out from the 'snug' area and sat at the bar next to us. 'Hi, Lottery Girl from...' I began, but then I forgot where it was that I had spoken to Mark. He said, 'From somewhere,' and then, with a big smile on his face, he took hold of my hand to shake it. 'From Hamburg,' I continued, before adding, 'Thank you so much for passing my message on to Gary,' and he said that was OK. While he waited to be served, I explained to him how in Stuttgart I had seen the VW vans drive off and I didn't mean to be on his floor when he was with his family, but he said that he didn't even remember the incident. I told him that I was sorry anyway, as I felt that I had invaded his personal space but he just said that it was already forgotten.

Lorraine asked him where she could go for a cigarette, but he

Mark and Howard laughing on stage at the Birmingham NEC.

said out of the front door was all he knew. Later, it was arranged for Mark to smoke from a door in the Cellar Bar so he did not have to keep going upstairs. A while later I saw Gary leaving the 'snug' and chatting to someone who was sitting by the entrance to it. By now, I was quite drunk and so, as he passed me, I caught his attention and then thanked him very much for Hamburg. He said, 'That's quite all right,' and then I told him to 'Have a good one' but I have no idea what I meant! Even though Mark was still up, I felt really tired and drunk, and so we decided to get a cab back to the Malmaison and call it a night.

The next day, when we returned to the Hotel du Vin at lunchtime, a man was already standing at the front door, asking whether you had a reservation or were a resident. We had booked a table for lunch in anticipation of this scenario and were escorted into the restaurant. There were plenty of girls in there already and also in the Bubble Bar situated on the ground floor, and of course the reception area. We smiled knowingly at them: we all knew why we were there! After lunch we found a small table with two chairs free and decided to sit there to see the guys gather to leave for the concert. There were about fifty girls standing outside the glass doors at the front of the hotel and possibly around another thirty moving about inside.

Howard came down before the others and he hung around in the lobby, chatting on his mobile. Girls were suddenly walking around in reception, some just standing and staring at him, which seemed very odd. He took a seat and then a hotel manager brought him a Mothercare bag for which he thanked him and then he went back upstairs. A while later, he came back down at about the same time as Gary and Dawn, and they chatted to James and Paul. There were so many girls crowded around in the lobby, and, when one decided to take a photo, she received a telling-off from Paul, who said that it was not acceptable inside the hotel. Had she never read the 'Stalking Take That In Hotels' handbook?

After they had got into one of the VWs, Jason came down the stairs and some fans that he must have known quite well rushed over to him; he spoke to them but then one asked for a photo and, although he agreed, he seemed very uncomfortable with it. The problem is that, if you start doing it for one, everyone else pushes forward wanting their turn, and, as this began to happen, Jason said, 'I have to go,' and headed towards the door.

Finally down the stairs was Mark to gasps from the crowd; someone said, 'Here comes the baby,' though I'm not going to comment because I too say some rather ridiculous things when I'm in their company! Mark made his way over to reception and said, 'See you Monday,' to the receptionist. I looked at Lorraine, who was already frowning at me. We were checking in tomorrow and it seemed like they were all checking out to enjoy their night off elsewhere!

We went back to the Malmaison to get ready for the evening; we were thinking that it would be pointless but nonetheless we still had to try. On our return, the du Vin was quiet and so we sat in the atrium area, drinking some wine. We wondered if we were going to see them tonight and speculated about what they might or might not decide to do.

At about 11 p.m., we saw Dawn in the reception and so we knew that at least Gary would be staying there tonight. We received a text from a friend, also staying at the hotel, telling us to come down to the Cellar Bar. Despite the fact that there was a sign at the entrance saying that it was closed for the evening, they had snuck down there only to find reserved signs on the 'snug'.

We immediately did as she said and slipped unnoticed down to the lower-ground-floor bar. It was quiet in there – only our friend, with all of her friends, and then Lorraine and me. There was, however, a bartender behind the bar, so it couldn't have been genuinely closed – had we struck gold? Time passed, and there was no sign of Gary, Howard or Jason, and it looked as though, even if they had planned to come down at some point to this bar, they had then changed their plans. When Lorraine went up for a cigarette, she was told by a girl outside that Gary and Howard had gone out shortly after returning to the hotel earlier.

At about 2 a.m., I decided that, even if they came back now, they would more than likely go to bed and not come down to the bar, and with that in mind we should just leave. As I came up the stairs to reception, the VW was just pulling up outside and, despite having been down in the bar for over three hours, I had picked exactly the right moment to come upstairs, remarkable timing! Gary, Dawn and Howard all came through reception and as Gary passed me he said, 'All right, love?' and I smiled.

Howard said to Gary, 'See you in a minute,' and so we went back down to the bar just in case he meant 'See you in a minute in the bar', but after half an hour we left and went back to the Malmaison.

The cruellest irony was that Gary and Howard had actually been at the Malmaison all night partying with the dancers and band and had we known we could, of course, have been in there too since we were residents! The next day, we checked into the Hotel du Vin, but it was eerily quiet in there – no fans outside, in the lobby or in the bar. This wasn't looking good. We checked their fake names at reception but now they had all checked out and would be returning the next day. We had a few drinks in the Bubble Bar and watched as the snow fell outside the window. This was rather unusual weather for that time of year and, just before we went to bed, some girls outside were having a snowball fight!

Lorraine had to leave early the next day for work and so I had invited my sister, Hayley, along to stay at the hotel with me that evening and come to the concert. She only lived twenty minutes away and arrived in the afternoon. I was incredibly excited about the concert that night because I had a front-row ticket. There is a website called the Take That Appreciation Pages which has been running for many years and has some message boards on there. One section was for people wanting to sell spare tickets but not wishing to support eBay. I had been on there looking for tickets when one was advertised for Birmingham; I asked which block and row and, when she answered block B, row A, I was stunned!

She sold the ticket for face value, not a penny more, and, when I met her to pay, I thanked her so much as she could have made a fortune from a ticket like that. I told Hayley that we would try to get her a last-minute one, just as we had all those years ago at the NEC, and then we could try to sneak her down to the front with me.

In the afternoon, we sat in the atrium area of the hotel, having a couple of drinks before leaving for the show. Next to us was another table of about seven girls and they were giggling as they got through a couple of bottles of wine. We saw Jason coming down the stairs and then he came into the atrium, smiled and said hello to everyone. For a moment, he chatted to someone just out of sight and then went over to the table of girls and asked if they were going to the show that evening and where they were sitting. Then he left for the concert and we quickly got ready and did the same.

At the NEC, we tried to join a queue for the box office but a steward told us we had no chance of getting tickets for that night's show, which really annoyed me because we *always* do! We called the box office instead and, when we got through, he said there was a ticket in block C that had become available. I thought this was good as C was next to B and it would be easier to get my sister to the front row. However, there was no need for this: the ticket that had become available was also in row A! Hayley couldn't believe it; she was so excited and I couldn't believe her luck.

Although I had been front row for a few of Gary's shows in the past, it was going to be so much more amazing to be

Howard dressed up for the dance section of the show.

front row at a Take That concert. After Sophie Ellis Bextor played her set, I was getting more and more excited about seeing the show from this position and Hayley was only a few seats away. The crowd started doing Mexican waves and the anticipation grew and grew. I kept checking the time; surely now the lights would go down? I just couldn't wait any longer! Then it happened and the show began, and, although I knew front row was going to be fantastic, I had no idea just how incredible it would be to watch the concert from that vantage point.

After the first couple of songs, Mark chatted to the crowd and said how things had changed over the years and how he was now the proud parent of a little boy, who was just taking his first steps. As he mimicked Elwood's wobbly attempts at walking, he said that it was reminiscent of him after a few too many drinks! Howard rather cruelly chipped in, 'Elwood's taller than you now, Markie!' and they were all laughing. As the guys walked over to the B stage, I laughed at the banner one woman was holding up that read, 'Tighter trousers please, Gary', as Lorraine and I had been saying for a while how tight his trousers always seemed to be.

After 'Back For Good', Mark was saying how great everyone's arm swaying had been and he seemed to go on about it for a bit. Then he pointed out one particular man in the crowd and said that he had been especially good at the arm waving. He invited the man on to the stage to show everyone how good he was at it and said that he might as well bring his lady up there with him too. I thought this was a very odd thing to do, but when he said, 'Everyone, this is Craig and Holly,' it was obvious something different was going on.

Mark went on to explain that they had received a letter from Craig, asking if he could do this, and with that Craig got down on one knee and the audience was cheering and clapping. We couldn't hear his proposal but it was obvious that Holly had said yes, and, as they hugged each other, Gary played 'A Million Love Songs'. Some of the people around me were actually crying and then, after Gary had finished playing, he got up and hugged Howard, and then everyone was hugging each other on the stage!

When the band returned to the main stage, Jason sang 'Wooden Boat' and, because I was so close, I could actually see just how nervous he was as he was about to sing. He explained how he struggled with being in the band and had been unsure whether or not to do the tour. 'Sometimes we don't know what we're waiting for, that's the time to be the first one on the dance floor,' and with that Jason ended his solo and the music pumped out for the energetic dance section and 'Give Good Feeling'. Normally, I leave not so long after that, but I couldn't waste any of my front-row position that night and so I got to see 'Never Forget' for the first time and 'Shine', which was outstanding!

I had told Hayley to come and meet me at the beginning of 'Pray' but then had to tear myself away so that we could get to the hotel! We had missed the train so we decided to jump in a cab back to the Hotel du Vin. Hayley was so excited; she told me that, as Mark had come back from the B stage through the crowd, she had grabbed his bum! She had been so in love with Mark when she was about eight, but had never met him in person. That night, she announced that she was going to tell him that as a child she had always thought he was 'the one' and I laughed.

When the guys arrived back at the hotel, they went to their rooms briefly and then returned to the reception, ready to go back out again. Gary saw me and said, 'I saw you in the front tonight,' and smiled.

I stuck up my thumb and said, 'Yeah, it was fantastic!'

There was a girl who was there by herself and I asked her to come and join us. She had followed the lads on Saturday night and she was the one who told me they had gone to the Malmaison. She went outside to take some photos of Howard as he left and then she said that she had to go home.

A while later, we got talking to two more girls, who were both very drunk but very excited that they might see Take That. They didn't have a room but they seemed nice enough and so I offered to get them a drink and allowed them to use my room key. As we chatted, we noticed that the two drivers had returned and so I decided to go and talk to one of them. He was standing at the reception desk and I made him the cheeky offer, 'I will give you £1,000 to tell me where you took the guys tonight.'

He replied, 'Sure, have you got it in cash?'

I told him that he wasn't supposed to say that and he should have refused, but he smiled and said that money was money.

It must have been past 2 a.m. when they finally went out to pick the guys up and, as I hadn't had any pictures with them so far, I decided to stand outside to wait for them to come back. There was only me, Hayley and one of the drunk girls (who was called Amy), as her friend had thrown up and passed out on the sofa in reception. Mark came back first and I asked if I could have a quick photo; he stopped and then went inside. Dawn had come back with Mark, so I thought this would be a good chance to get a photo with Gary too when he came back.

Howard was next to return and Amy had declared him her favourite. She said to him, 'Howard, have you heard this?' and he replied, 'What's that, love?' and she told him, 'I'm getting married next week.' He congratulated her, then she said, 'Erm, Howard, don't you remember you're supposed to be meeting me at the other end of the aisle!'

I took their picture and explained to a bemused, yet smiling Howard that she was extremely drunk!

Soon after, Gary returned and I asked him for a 'sneaky one' and turned my camera to face us for a quick photo – I hate asking, but then, if you remain constantly polite, you'll never get anything! He didn't seem to mind and then posed for one with Hayley after I had introduced him to her. I told him that I would see him in Glasgow and he smiled and said, 'God bless you!' and went inside.

Finally, the last one back was Jason, quite a bit later than the others. I too asked him for a 'sneaky one' but, when Amy and her friend (who had come out from the sofa to call a taxi for them both) began to speak to him, he became quite mean and asked, 'Why are you even standing here? Haven't you got anything better to do?'

I looked at my sister with raised eyebrows; I understood it was late but I had never before heard a member of Take That be cruel to fans like that. Feeling quite horrible, Amy explained that they were staying at the hotel and Jason snapped, 'Why don't you go inside then?'

I felt sorry for the girls – although they were being drunk and a bit silly, they were really lovely and didn't deserve that at all.

Me with Jason at the Hotel du Vin, Birmingham.

I said to Jason that, although he didn't understand it, we *did* think it was worth it to stand outside or sit inside, whichever the case might be, and that maybe he just didn't comprehend his own worth. With that we compromised, and he agreed to a group photo with the other three, rather than individual shots, and then he went inside. The girls' taxi arrived and they left. With the guys seemingly having all gone to bed, we went to our room to get some sleep.

The next morning I checked out of the hotel and stayed that night at my mother's house nearby, where I managed to get some clothes washed and have some rest before the long drive up to Glasgow. Thanks, Mum!

The following morning, it was back on the road and up to the rather lovely (and rather expensive) Mar Hall hotel on the outskirts of Glasgow, near Erskine Bridge. I was delighted to have been given a room with a window overlooking the entrance to the hotel as it meant less time sitting in reception just to figure out who was coming into the hotel or leaving. Mr M Anthony was booked in for four nights from the Wednesday and so I sat at the table by the window making use of the free Internet, having a glass of wine and enjoying the view!

First to arrive was Jason with James, Paul and Chris Healey, and then a while later Howard pulled up in his snazzy Range Rover. There didn't appear to be any other fans at the hotel, which was both exciting and scary, but in the end it didn't matter as neither Mark nor Gary showed up, and after spending a couple of hours in the bar it was clear that the other two were not going to make an appearance either.

The next day we had some tea in the Grand Hall of the hotel and then watched from the window as Howard went out to speak to fans and have some photos taken before leaving for the show with the others, who made a dash for the VW. While Take That were at the SECC for another sell-out concert, we made full use of the swimming pool and spa area of the hotel. We were too afraid to use it during the day in case any of the guys were in there, not wanting to invade their privacy in the pool (even though it is open to *all* residents, it felt odd) but also because we couldn't face seeing them in our swimsuits with our wobbly bits hanging out!

After our swim, we went back up to the room to get ready for the evening ahead. There, we drank as much of our own alcohol as we could before we had to pay the exorbitant prices in the bar. We had three choices of where to sit downstairs: there was a residents-only room at the front of the hotel which offered us a view of the entrance so that we could see the guys returning, the Grand Hall running through the middle of the hotel, like an enlarged reception area, and the bar which was beautiful, but very small. We opted for the residents' room, where we practically had to whisper to each other, it was so quiet!

Shortly after 11 p.m., the silver VWs pulled up and we heard the guys walking through reception. Chris Healey came into the room and discussed with another woman whether they should have some drinks there, commenting on the amazing view from the window of the river and the hills. They left, and then Jason came in, smiled and left again. Shortly afterwards, Mark entered. He walked to our table and said, 'Hello.'

I replied, 'Hi, sorry it's me again.' I'm not sure why I was apologising but I think the way Jason had spoken to us the other night had made me feel quite bad!

The guys (minus Gary) ended up in the bar anyway, with Jason sharing one table with footballer Gary Neville and some other friends, Mark was on a table with some fans and Howard sat at the only other table at the back with James, Paul and Jeremy, who had been described to me as the tour physiotherapist. We stayed in the residents' room at the front for a while and then went into the bar to get some drinks, then decided just to stay there and stand at the bar.

Once Howard, James and Paul had left, I went to ask Jeremy if he minded if we sat at the table with him and he said that was fine. We started a conversation in which he described his role on the tour as physiotherapist, spiritual counsellor, part-time security and personal assistant – a bit of everything! I have always been interested in all matters spiritual and, over the next hour or so, we had a lovely conversation about the meaning of life, with Mark still on the table next to us with about six or seven fans, who were buying rosé wine and cocktails for him to enjoy. It was clear that he was becoming more and more drunk until eventually he stared at the drinks in front of him and said, 'Help me!'

At around 3 a.m., Mark, some of the girls he had been sitting with and Lorraine went out of a side door leading out from the Grand Hall to have a cigarette. It was very cold outside and Mark was asking for 'huddles and cuddles' from the girls to keep warm. The look on Lorraine's face when she came back was a picture! She said that Mark had asked her for a cuddle and he had rested his head on her as they smoked and that she couldn't believe how lovely he was!

As she was describing to me how soft his hair was, we heard a Take That song being played on the piano in the Grand Hall and we guessed it might be Mark. A few moments later, we heard a woman telling him off and saying that it was too late for him to play; he came back to the bar and rejoined the girls at the table.

I continued talking to Jeremy until at about 3.30 a.m. Mark stood up and began giving all the girls he was sitting with a goodnight hug. I hadn't expected him to come over to Lorraine and me, but was delighted when he walked over to us with his arms out. As I hugged him, I said, 'Thank you, Mark,' and kissed his cheek, as I thought that it had been very sweet of him to include us before he left.

Lorraine went to bed and I carried on talking to Jeremy until about 4 a.m. I told him that I missed speaking to Gary, as I had done on the previous tours, and recounted to him some of the fun we had had before.

The next day Lorraine and I went out to nearby Clydebank to get some supplies and get a hangover-busting McDonalds for lunch. When we returned to the hotel, we sat in the Grand Hall and ordered some tea. At around 3 p.m., Gary walked through, looking gorgeous in a tight dark-grey T-shirt, making me feel even sadder that this tour was not affording us the opportunities to have a chat or a laugh like his old tours used to do. As he walked past us again shortly after, he said, 'Hello, how are you?' We smiled and said 'hello' back.

When Gary came back through, he was with Dawn again and they headed to the residents' room at the front of the hotel, which now had a sign on it reading 'Private'. Howard and Jason soon followed and joined Gary, Dawn and other tour entourage in the room. Finally, Mark came through and walked over to our table. 'Good morning, Mark!' I began, and then laughed because it was actually well into the afternoon. He laughed and then turned to the girls he had sat with the night before and said, 'Thanks for the drinks, girls, but not the hangover!' He went off to join the others and soon they left for the show.

That evening the 'Private' sign still hung on the door to the residents' room and we had a feeling they would be spending the night in there. We found a table in the bar and were joined by two women, who were out celebrating. Earlier in the day, they had been very excited to suddenly see Take That walk past them in the Grand Hall and asked if we thought they might come into the bar that night. We tried to explain that we never knew just what kind of night it was going to be and how one minute you might be sitting at the same table enjoying drinks with one of the band and the next not get a word at all. They listened intently as we recounted some stories of the times we had spent with Gary and then they decided to go down to the residents' room to see what was happening.

When they returned, they said that Gary had already gone to bed, having walked by not long ago with Dawn, and wished everyone goodnight. I went to the toilet and, as I returned to the bar, I bumped into Mark, who was also on his way in there.

I warned him, 'Lay off those cocktails tonight, Mark!' and he laughed. I asked him if he had been OK for the show and he said, 'Yeah, fine.'

Once in the bar, the girls from the previous night also came in and they took the same table as they had the night before. Again, Mark joined them. I was feeling quite tired and so I suggested to Lorraine that I come with her while she went for a cigarette.

We went out of the front entrance to the hotel, then stood at the bottom of the steps; it was absolutely freezing but was doing the intended job of waking me up a bit! After Lorraine had finished her cigarette, she went back inside and I told her I would be back in soon. When I turned to go back inside, I saw that Mark was heading my way and, although not the most subtle thing I have ever done, I turned back round and waited for him by the steps. I totally blame the alcohol for being so blatant!

Mark lit a cigarette and I felt that I needed a reason to be standing there and so I asked him if he had a spare one. He opened up his packet and gave me a Marlboro Light, then lit it for me with his lighter. I told him that I hadn't smoked a cigarette in 16 months and said that it must be the excitement of seeing all the guys in the hotel. He said that he had tried to give up, but had only made it to the three-month point before lighting up again. I told him that, despite standing there with a cigarette in my hand, it had taken me nine to ten months to be truly over the habit. Mark then shared his intention to quit in the New Year and said, 'If you see me with one of these in my hand next year, can you hit me?' and we laughed.

I told him that I had met him loads of times over the years but that he probably didn't recognise me because it had been so spread out. I reminded him of the time I had been inside Abbey Road and how he had come to borrow £3 from me for cigarettes and how I had felt bad for being in there, but he told me it was all right and not to worry. I said that I knew Gary much better and was disappointed because he kept going up to bed! Mark explained, 'It's because he's got his lady with him,' and I smiled knowingly. With that, and the disgusting cigarette smoked, we went back inside.

Just as we were deciding to call it a night, we saw Mark walking around by reception, annoyed at himself because he had left his key in his room and was locked out! He had to wait for the receptionist to return to let him into his room. As we passed, we wished him goodnight and then went to bed.

Another day, another hangover! I apologised to my body for what I was putting it through, especially as, when I woke up, I remembered having smoked a cigarette and I decided to spend the day relaxing in the room. Lorraine went down to the Grand Hall to see the guys gather in reception ready to leave for the show and she promised that she would keep me up to date by text message! There was a wedding taking place at the hotel in the afternoon and I could hear the sound of bagpipes being played by the entrance as guests left to go to a separate building that was to house the reception.

Just as the guests were making their way through, Mark inadvertently stepped out into them and Lorraine described how security guard Paul literally pushed him out of the way so

MAD ABOUT THE BOYS

as not to disturb the couple's happy day with fans trying to get to Mark! Once it was clear, the guys were free to get into the VWs, posing briefly for a few photos with their fans, and then they left for the final show in Glasgow.

Once they had gone, we decided to go to Braehead Shopping and Leisure Centre to have a look at some clothes as we seemed to have exhausted all our outfits! I found a gorgeous black dress in Wallis and Lorraine bought some black skinny jeans and a grey top to go with them. As this was the last concert in Glasgow, and with a night off the following day, maybe the guys would be in a party mood and maybe, just maybe Gary might actually talk to us that night?

We returned to the hotel to get ready and then decided to sit in the Grand Hall area. Once more, the residents' room was labelled 'Private' and the bar was being used by some of the wedding guests that had come up from the reception. As they walked through the Grand Hall (being very drunk, as all good wedding guests are), they made stupid comments like, 'Oh yeah, I heard that Howard was the gay one' or 'Yes, that band Take That are here tonight' to try to wind us up.

The band themselves were not privy to this teasing as they had gone out to exclusive private members' club 29 for the evening, leaving us to sit and wait for their return. Howard came back first and went up to his room, and then we overheard Jeremy trying to persuade him to come down to the residents' room for a drink – a request we all shared. When Gary returned and walked past me with Dawn, he winked and said, 'See ya, love,' before wishing the girls on the other table goodnight. I felt very sad that he was going to bed yet again; all I wanted was a few minutes to have a chat like we used to, but it seemed as if things were never going to be that good again.

After a while, Howard did decide to come back down and began chatting to us about his evening. He said that he'd had a massage in the hope of becoming tired enough to get some sleep; however, it had had the opposite effect and had woken him up completely. We talked about the hotel and how it used to be a hospital, with one section originally a morgue, and how it might be haunted. One girl said to Howard, 'Robbie used to see ghosts, didn't he?' and Howard wittily replied, 'No, love, that was the drugs!' We were all really laughing and then one of the other girls pulled out a DVD that she had made of all Jason's bits of the Channel 4 TV series *Killer Net*. She asked if Howard would pass it on to him but he said, 'Naaah,' and laughed.

Talk then turned to Howard's injury and how he was feeling, and he told us that he had not been able to do a back flip since it happened and that it was rather like getting back on a horse after a fall, but that he hadn't managed to do it yet.

Some cheeky girl then turned to him and said, 'Well, you are getting a bit old for this now, Howard!'

He laughed and said, 'Yes, we won't do it again!'

He chatted for a while longer, talking about films and how much he loved *A Beautiful Mind* starring Russell Crowe, and then he said that he was going to go and get some sleep.

Finally, Mark returned somewhere around 3 a.m. and came

over to say hello to us, though it was clear that he had had more than a few drinks! He joined Jeremy in the residents' room but soon came back out to sit with us and chat about the evening and where he had been. The Stereophonics were due to arrive at about 4 a.m. and Mark said that he was going to stay up to meet them, so we started teasing him about acting like a fan and asking if he wanted us to take his picture with Kelly Jones! We spotted the tour bus pulling up at the front of the hotel and told Mark that they were here. He asked how we knew and I said, 'We're experts at this!' at which he started laughing.

Mark went out of the hotel for a cigarette and to greet the band as they came in and then they all went into the residents' room for a few drinks. Shortly afterwards, he came over to us again and said that he was very tired but that it wasn't very rock'n'roll of him to tell the Stereophonics that he was going to bed! He started saying, 'Come on, Mark, you can do it!' and we were all laughing so much at him, as he was clearly very drunk. We told him that he could perhaps throw something out of the window if he wanted to be a bit more rock'n'roll. Someone then shouted, 'Do a Liam Gallagher swagger!' So Mark began walking down the Grand Hall, pretending he was Liam Gallagher, and we gave him a round of applause. Incidentally, it was a very good impression!

At about 4.30 a.m., I was practically falling asleep and so I decided to go outside to get some fresh air with Lorraine as she went for a cigarette and was happy to see Mark coming down the steps after us, this time without my having to do an obvious about-turn! He was joined by a couple, who had been guests at the wedding and who had somehow got into the residents' room and were drinking with Mark and the Stereophonics. The man was extremely drunk and had come past us at one point, bragging about how Mark was buying his drinks, which we found very distasteful.

This man began to talk to me and asked how old I was. I told him to guess and he said, 'Twenty-five.'

I said that I was incredibly flattered because I was actually 31, and Mark, who had been listening, said, 'You look very well on it,' making my year with that comment! Mark then asked me where I lived and I told him Brighton, which he said he thought was lovely. The drunk man then asked Mark where he lived and I thought he wouldn't want to answer with two fans standing there but he went ahead and told the man the part of London he now lived in, saying that he had lived in the Lake District for ten years, but no longer had a house there.

Then the guy, who was by now staggering a bit, was up close to Mark and said, 'I went to see a tribute band to Take That once – they were a punk band and were called "Take This You C**t"!' Mark smiled and I was laughing at this man's story, which went on, 'They did "Relight My Fire" and they sang, "Gonna set the fucking bus stop on fire!"'

Mark laughed politely and I was in absolute stitches, seeing the incredibly drunk wedding guest telling him this story.

We went back inside and, since we were all starving, we ordered some plates of sandwiches to keep us going as Mark was clearly going to be up for some time. I also stopped drinking alcohol and switched to water at this point, knowing I had a long drive ahead the next day. As we were enjoying our late-night munch, Mark came through to the Grand Hall to ask us if he could still walk in a straight line and then he practised walking up and down. He could just about manage it and so we told him that he was doing OK. At about 6 a.m., he told us that he was finally going to bed, only to return five minutes later because once again he had locked himself out of his room! The receptionist was nowhere to be seen and Mark was telling himself off for being so stupid two nights in a row. We offered to help him find the woman and had a look around until we saw her coming out of a room, then we called out to him that we had found her. He thanked us, and told us we were very rock'n'roll for still being up, but then was taken to his room for the second time in as many days by the receptionist!

The next morning I woke, feeling really tired, and not only were we checking out that day but we were also driving all the way to Newcastle! We loaded up the car and then went to the restaurant for Sunday lunch, which was very expensive but absolutely fantastic. Honeyed parsnip soup with chilli, warm bread rolls and lamb with all the trimmings! Just what we needed to make us feel ready for the drive ahead. Mark had told us that he was looking forward to having lunch there that afternoon but I wanted to get mine eaten and get out of there before the lads took their table, as I felt too hungover and fragile to deal with the nerves of seeing them! When we rejoined the other girls in the Grand Hall, they had some bad news: a member of staff at the hotel (who had so far given correct information) had informed them that Take That had changed their plans and now they were not going to Newcastle, but staying at Mar Hall instead for another day. There wasn't much that we could do – our room at the Newcastle Malmaison could not be cancelled and Mar Hall was fully booked anyway.

As we contemplated what to do and what time we should leave, Gary and Dawn came down for lunch. Gary looked very smart in an expensive-looking black-and-brown jumper and black trousers, but he didn't say anything. I said it wasn't surprising that we hadn't seen Mark yet today but someone said that in fact they *had* seen him at 10 a.m. for breakfast – as no one else had been around, he went back upstairs again.

If we could have had a room there that night, would we have been crazy enough to book it and have two rooms to pay for? Quite possibly, but all the fans were leaving that day so just Lorraine and I sitting there would look a bit silly anyway and it was a bit intrusive. Perhaps we needed a night off and to get some sleep in Newcastle and maybe the guys could also do with a night off and to have some space to enjoy the hotel without us lot!

Hard as it was, we left at about 3 p.m. and began the drive to Newcastle. We were meeting Lucy and Debbie there and they were none too pleased when we told them the guys were staying in Glasgow! Arriving at the Malmaison brought back so many memories: the first time Gary had come to sit with us and the waitress coming over and asking us if we wanted a drink, courtesy of Gary Barlow; his second tour and the night spent in the bar laughing at his awful and distasteful jokes, and the lift where I had stupidly told him about my dream, which still made me cringe as I took my luggage up to my room.

Despite the disappointment, it was lovely to see Lucy and Debbie again and we went to a nearby Italian restaurant for dinner and talked about old times. When we returned, I apologised, but said that a certain someone had kept me up past 6 a.m. and that I needed some sleep! I gave myself a relatively early night for a change.

We had been told by some of the other fans we knew that the next day Take That would be going straight from Glasgow to the venue in Newcastle and so we would not see them until the evening. Even so, the girls wanted to go out for lunch and then wait in reception just in case. I was just getting ready in the room when I realised that I had left one of my bags in the car and that it had my make-up in it. It was around 3.30 p.m. and I thought that could be dangerous timing to walk around with a bare face, but I reminded myself that they were going straight to the venue so I would be fine.

As I stepped out into reception, I immediately saw Jeremy and huge amounts of luggage with Take That signs on it, waiting to go up to the relevant rooms. 'Oh, dear Lord, get me to my car!' I thought, as I tried to escape out the back door to the car park opposite. I called Lorraine, who said that the guys had arrived about ten minutes earlier and that she was going to have a look to see which entrance the VWs were parked at, to know where they were going to leave from.

I managed to get back up to the room without bumping

into anyone and set about drying my hair and doing my face before joining the others downstairs. By now, there were lots of girls in reception, all waiting for Take That to come down and leave for the show. The only table left was a small two-seater directly opposite the lifts. It really couldn't have been any more blatant, but I said, 'Come on, it's our last day, who cares? They know why we're here!' and tried to make a joke of it.

First down was Jason, who went straight out of the back door and was gone. Next it was Howard, who did smile and say hello as he came through and then went to stand with James and Paul to wait for the others. I had bumped into Paul on the corridor and he had asked me if I was following him but, since I had been at the hotel first, I argued that it was in fact he who was following me! The next one down was Gary, who commented as the lift doors opened to tables full of girls, 'This looks like the right place!' and he went to join Howard. About five minutes later, Mark came down and said hello and then Lucy excitedly told him that she had a front-row ticket for the show that night and that he should look out for her banner, which he said he would. He went to join Gary and Howard and some of the dancers, who were actually staying at the same hotel for a change. Then they went out the back of the hotel, through the fans and even some paparazzi, and off to the show.

That evening, things looked promising in the bar when upon entering we noticed that half of it was sectioned off as 'reserved'. We took the nearest table to the reserved section and, as promised, held on to some seats for Lucy, Debbie and their friends for when they returned from the concert.

After 11 p.m., some dancers and musicians came into the bar and the fantastic singer Lloyd Wade went around, saying hello to people, who were only too happy to speak to him. Support act Sophie Ellis Bextor was also in the bar that night with her band, so it was looking like it might be quite an evening.

The first one of Take That down to the bar was Howard, looking gorgeous in a cream jumper, who took a large table by the window with manager Jonathan, while security James and Paul sat on stools nearby. Mark came down next and joined Howard, although, as is usual for Mark, he also made his way round the 'non-Take That' side of the bar to say hello to people and spend some time asking them if they had enjoyed the show. Gary came down with Dawn and they also sat with Howard, and then Jason arrived and sat at a separate table with some of the dancers.

When Mark came over to say hello to us, I couldn't help but share my disappointment with him that it was to be my last night, and, despite having spent so much time with Gary in the past, now it seemed as if he couldn't even spare a few moments to say more than 'hello' to me. Again, Mark said that Gary wasn't able to talk to anyone because Dawn was with him, and it was true that, when Mark had his fiancée Emma with him, he didn't spend time with the fans in the same way as he had been doing in her absence. I understood, but it was a hard thing to take, especially after being so close to feel so ignored.

Mark went back over to join Gary and Howard and I chatted

to the girls, who were making the most of being together again on tour. We enjoyed some wine and had a laugh until the early hours but then, upset at it being my last night, I decided to go outside for a cigarette with Lucy, only to find Mark standing there having one too. He asked me what I was drinking and, when I told him it was a rosé wine spritzer, he took my glass and began drinking some! We chatted as we smoked and I told him how I had enjoyed talking to Jeremy in Glasgow after he had described himself as a spiritual counsellor and mentioned some of the books that I had enjoyed in the same sort of genre that Mark had heard of and also liked. Lucy spoke to him about the show and about how my nickname for her is the 'Mark expert' and he was laughing.

Back in the bar, I told Mark that I wanted to thank him for taking the time to talk to us and that it really did mean so much. I explained that, when I had received the hotel bill for Mar Hall (totalling nearly £1,000), I would have thrown up if it wasn't for him but that he had made it all worth it. With that, he said, 'Come here,' and put his arms out and we hugged. I thanked him again and told him that I meant it from the heart.

With the long drive home to Brighton in front of me the next day I decided to go to bed. I said goodnight to all of the girls, old friends and some new that I had met on this tour. I was glad to be going home, but sad too that it was all over. I know the band don't owe us anything outside of the albums or concerts they produce and that we pay for, but I still felt very sad that, having spent so much time with Gary in the past, he didn't find the time to come and say a few words to us, his most loyal fans, at some point over the 12 days we had spent on the tour with the band. For now, though, it was over and all we could do was hope that this would not be the end and that maybe the guys had one more tour in them for us to enjoy in the not too distant future! Well, here's hoping...

DISCOGRAPHIES

TAKE THAT DISCOGRAPHY

ALBUMS

Album title	Released	Highest UK Chart Position
Take That and Party	August 1992	2
Everything Changes	October 1993	1
Nobody Else	May 1995	1
Greatest Hits	May 1996	1
The Ultimate Collection	November 2005	2
Beautiful World	November 2006	1

SINGLES

Single Title	Released	Highest UK Chart Position
Do What U Like	July 1991	82
Promises	November 1991	38
Once You've Tasted Love	January 1992	47
It Only Takes A Minute	May 1992	7

MAD ABOUT THE BOYS

I Found Heaven	August 1992	15
A Million Love Songs	September 1992	7
Could It Be Magic	December 1992	3
Why Can't I Wake Up With You	February 1993	2
Pray	July 1993	1
Relight My Fire	September 1993	1
Babe	December 1993	1
Everything Changes	March 1994	1
Love Ain't Here Anymore	July 1994	3
Sure	October 1994	1
Back For Good	March 1995	1
Never Forget	July 1995	1
How Deep Is Your Love	March 1996	1
Patience	November 2006	1
Shine	February 2007	1
I'd Wait For Life	June 2007	17
Rule The World	October 2007	2

GARY BARLOW DISCOGRAPHY

ALBUMS

Album Title	Released	Highest UK Chart Position
Open Road	June 1997	1
Twelve Months, Eleven Days	October 1999	35

SINGLES

Single Title	Released	Highest UK Chart Position
Forever Love	July 1996	1
Love Won't Wait	April 1997	1
So Help Me Girl	July 1997	11
Open Road	November 1997	7
Stronger	July 1999	16
For All That You Want	September 1999	24

ROBBIE WILLIAMS DISCOGRAPHY

ALBUMS

Album Title	Released	Highest UK Chart Position
Life Thru A Lens	September 1997	1
I've Been Expecting You	October 1998	1
Sing When You're Winning	August 2000	1
Swing When You're Winning	November 2001	1
The Ego Has Landed	July 2002	1
Escapology	November 2002	1
Live at Knebworth	September 2003	2
Greatest Hits	October 2004	1
Intensive Care	October 2005	1
Rudebox	October 2006	1

SINGLES

Single Title	Released	Highest UK Chart Position
Freedom	August 1996	2
Old Before I Die	April 1997	2
Lazy Days	July 1997	8
South of the Border	September 1997	14
Angels	December 1997	4
Let Me Entertain You	March 1998	3
Millennium	September 1998	1
No Regrets	November 1998	4
Strong	March 1999	4
She's the One	November 1999	1

DISCOGRAPHY

Rock DJ	July 2000	1
Kids	September 2000	2
Supreme	December 2000	4
Let Love Be Your Energy	April 2001	10
Eternity/Road to Mandalay	July 2001	1
Somethin' Stupid	December 2001	1
Feel	December 2002	2
Come Undone	March 2003	4
Something Beautiful	July 2003	3
Sexed Up	November 2003	10
Radio	October 2004	1
Misunderstood	December 2004	8
Tripping	October 2005	2
Advertising Space	December 2005	8
Sin Sin Sin	May 2006	22
Rudebox	September 2006	4
Lovelight	November 2006	8
She's Madonna	March 2007	16

MARK OWEN DISCOGRAPHY

ALBUMS

Album Title	Released	Highest UK Chart Position
Green Man	December 1996	33
In Your Own Time	November 2003	59
How the Mighty Fall	April 2005	0

SINGLES

Single Title	Released	Highest UK Chart Position
Child	November 1996	3
Clementine	February 1997	3
I Am What I Am	August 1997	29
Four Minute Warning	August 2003	4
Alone With You	October 2003	26
Makin' Out	June 2004	30
Believe In the Boogie	August 2005	57
Hail Mary	January 2006	103